THE NEXT WORLD

Poems by 32 Third World Americans

Edited by Joseph Bruchac

The Crossing Press
Trumansburg, New York

ACKNOWLEDGMENTS:

poems by Michael Harper from *New Letters*
poems by Gary Soto: *Field Poem* from *The Greenfield Review; Town* and *Hoeing* from *The Iowa Review; Remember* from *The Nation.*
poems by Mbembe: *The World is a Stubbed Toe* and *Something Else They Say* from *Chateau Review; High* published in *To Go On,* BKMK Press, 1973.
poems by Thulani: *Forest Green* published in *Jambalaya,* Reed, Cannon & Johnson; *Song for Nkazi* published in *Time To Greez,* Glide Publications.

We wish to thank the poets in this anthology for the manuscript use of their poems.

Cover & graphics by Karl Wolff
(cover drawing is the Hopi people's symbol of emergence)

The Crossing Press Series of Contemporary Anthologies

Library of Congress Cataloging in Publication Data
Main entry under title:

The Next world.

(The Crossing Press series of contemporary anthologies)
1. American poetry--Minority authors.
2. American poetry--20th century. I. Bruchac, Joseph, 1942-
PS591.M54N44 811'.5'408 78-1923
ISBN 0-89594-008-6
ISBN 0-89594-009-4 pbk.

CONTENTS

INTRODUCTION

Three years ago, on the campus of a small Wisconsin college, the events which were the genesis of this anthology took place. There, at Stevens Point, a group of writers gathered from all over the United States to take part in a workshop sponsored by the National Center For Audio Experimentation. All of them were young, all of them were members of ethnic minorities, and all of them found out that the similarities of their experiences and interests far outweighed the differences. Ed Burrows, himself a talented poet and the initiator of the idea of this two week long workshop, had brought together some of the most vital young writers in America, and in introducing them to each other strengthened and initiated connections which are still rocking the literary world. A special issue of *The Greenfield Review* featuring the poets of the NCAE conference appeared in January 1974.

Although the NCAE workshop was a one-shot deal, lightning struck again in May 1974 in the town of Ellensburg, Washington, where the Japanese American poet, Alex Kuo, put together a Third World Arts Workshop Festival which brought some of those who had been at the Stevens Point Conference (which was already a sort of minor legend) with a number of other equally exciting Third World Writers: James Welch, Ishmael Reed, Victor Hernandez Cruz, Al Young and Rudolfo Anaya. Neil Parsons, a painter who has made good use of his Blackfeet ancestry in his work was also a participant in that week-long conference, and by the time the week was over, a week which saw over 100 high school and college students take part in workshops led by the writers mentioned above, Neil Parsons found himself writing poetry along with everyone else. It was that kind of an experience.

From those two conferences came the idea for this anthology, an anthology which is different from most traditional anthologies. We are living in a time of many anthologies, a time when Daniel Halpern's *The American Poetry Anthology* (which includes some of the writers already mentioned) seems about to be the mid-seventies most publicized answer to Paul Carroll's *The Young American Poets* of the sixties. There is also a current trend to bring out "Theme" anthologies, collections which draw their contributors from a narrowly defined group such as Native Americans or Women (in the sixties it was Blacks) or a region, such as Michigan or Fresno. There are both good and bad things about this flood of anthologies. The bad things are perhaps the most obvious -- that some collections are pure rip-offs, thrown hastily together by publishers who want to bring out *their* Indian anthology before the market is glutted, that too often an anthology is slanted in such a way as to influence a reader into thinking that that anthology is *the* anthology. The good things, which may be less obvious, include the fact that this is an era which is alive with exciting new poets, a new era in which voices which have been traditionally silent (or silenced) are being heard.

In a way, *The Next World* can be seen as a thematic anthology, if we can accept as a theme the idea that differences produce similarities...which still remain very different. It is a collection of younger poets, Chinese-American, Chicano, Afro-American, Puerto Rican, Filipino, Native American, Japanese-American men and women from vastly different backgrounds who are fine poets and, as much as any poet in the anthologies mentioned above, *Americans*.

All of the poets in this anthology have felt, usually first hand, the prejudice which is part of the American experience. All of them have risen above it by making literature out of it, not "just protest literature" (as if to protest is to make writing immediately invalid) or poems written according to easy political formulas, but work which is both lasting and original. Just compare the syncopated rhythms of Jesus Papoleto Melendez's *Willie Bobo was a Baad Dude* with Ricardo Sanchez's *Drum.* Here are two poems by writers with a Latin background, two poems about the experience of being different in America, and two poems which could not be more different.

A number of the poets included in this collection were not at Stevens Point or Ellensburg. Many of them are women, for there was an imbalance at both conferences -- a reflection of the fact that if ethnic writers have been neglected and women have been neglected, then it stands to reason that Third World women have been *doubly* neglected. Jessica Hagedorn, who is a quiet revolution all by herself, introduced some of these writers to me and I am grateful. She, Ntozake Shange, Thulani, Nashira Ntosha, Alma Villanueva and Janet Hale are welcome additions, as are Alan Chong Lau, Pancho Aguilar and Tony Moreno, writers who have, in recent months contributed work to *The Greenfield Review*. Additionally, Ron Welburn and Sandra Maria Esteves, "alumni" of Stevens Point are included.

Ever since the great Bandung conference of more than two decades ago we have heard a great deal about the "Third World", the phrase that was coined to refer to those nations which were not in either the communist bloc or the capitalist. In the last year or two we have begun hearing of the "Fourth World" and even the "Fifth World", those nations which are so impoverished as to be out of the sphere of influence which the "Third World" sways. We have seen in recent years that the "Third World" also exists within the borders of the United States. We are a nation of nations, some of them as unnoticed as the Armenians, some as visible as the Black Americans, and some whose boundaries were established by Federal and state statutures. (How many people know, for example, of the existence of the Seneca Republic in New York State, a self-governing Native American nation?) Native American people have always felt a good deal of reticence about speaking of the "Third World." According to the legends of most of the original inhabitants of this Turtle Continent, their people have passed through a number of worlds to come to this one. The Hopis speak of the First World which was left behind to enter the Second World, which was left behind to enter the Third World, which was left behind. By the reckoning of the Navajo people, they are now in the Fifth World. And as each world was left behind, destroyed by the forces of corruption and misdeeds, a new world was found, one in which the chances of a better way still existed.

When the Paiute holy man Kwohitsauq, who was also known as Wovoka, became the prophet of the Ghost Dance he prophesied that the deeds and the buildings of the whites would be wiped off the land, everything made new again, the buffalo returning, the people given a new world.

The poets in this anthology all have one thing in common. In their poems they have given us not just criticism of this flawed world of Watergates and intervention in Angola, of assassinations and racial repression, they have also given us visions -- of the almost forgotten past, of the present and its possibilities, of the promise of the future. They are not just "poets of the seventies" or spokes-people for some special group, they are human beings whose poems point us towards a better future, roads to the next world.

Maka' sito'maniyan ukiye
Oya'te uki'ye oya'te uki'ye,
Wa'nbli oya'te wan hoshi'hi-ye lo,
Ata heye lo, ate heye lo,
Maka o'wancha'ya uki'ye.

The whole world is coming,
A nation is coming, a nation is coming,
The Eagle has brought the message to the people,
The father says so, the father says so,
Over the whole Earth they are coming.

(from the Dakota)

Joseph Bruchac

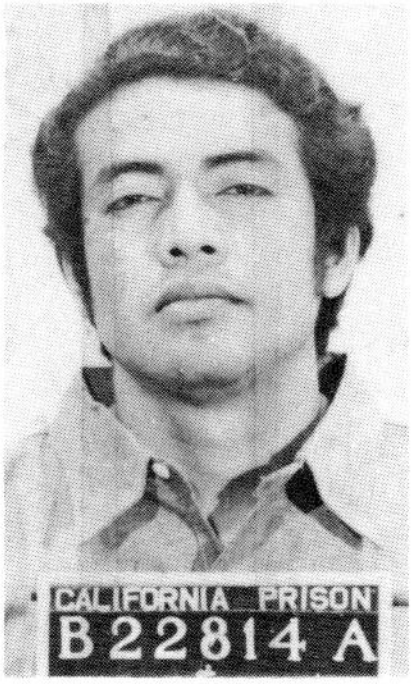

Pancho Aguila

I was born in the year of 1945, the year that atomic bombs were unleashed upon the world's people. My birthland is Nicaragua but my life experiences since the age to two have been the United State. I am a product of San Francisco's streets, counter-culture attitudes and ideas and the social class struggle. I have been locked up in California's most stringent prisons for the last seven years of my life except for a brief escape period in 1972. My sentence is life imprisonment. I am still relegated to cage 857, Folsom State Prison.

Poetry became a real light to me in the Haight-Ashbury of 1967 at which time I wrote poetry and read at a few readings. The revolutionary consciousness of that period destined me to prison. I wrote at first in prison but became disillusioned when officials interpreted my poetry as inciting to riot and it was used as evidence to send me to the "hole". I stopped writing when fifty or more poems turned up missing in a shakedown. The guards were angry because of a general strike and when I asked about my work no one knew anything. Since 1972 the Supreme Court has ruled in our favor and has set down laws to protect writers but needless to say harassment occurs to the degree of one's unpopularity with the state. I now write to express what is demanding release from within.

Publications: 1) *Poets and Writers in Folsom Prison* by Gypsy Table V: Special Issue; 2) *Echoes Off the Walls I & II* by Fault Publications; 3) *Captive Voices* by Dustbooks; 4) *Second Coming, Vol. 3, No. 3* by Second Coming Press; 5) *Tin Tan* by Pocho Che, San Francisco, California.

HAPPY BIRTHDAY AMERICA

Today
I am one-thousand, nine-hundred & seventy-five years old
Thats right I'm starting from zero
Like a flat halo of an angel
Or the disc of an olympic thrower
I start with a zero stamped on my forehead
I begin with the nothingness of existence
Like the shadows of a prison cell
I begin with the egg
Resurrected before the masses
Frenzic with the cry for blood
(thats right!)
I begin in the year of a circle
In the shape of a garbage top
Or the rabbit hole, alice fell into
I begin at the top of the trap of the sink
At the origin of the spiralling zero of the whirlpool
Today
I am one-thousand, nine-hundred & seventy-five years old
I wear the shirt of centuries soiled with blood
I wear wings of laughter, a balloon that cannot be tied down
As well as a tear that now fills oceans
For all who came n went without a splash or word
Quiet moccasins across the forest floor
I wear the shoes of stars
Numerous like the milkyway
Size 12D to 5B, baby shoes n wooden ones n barefeet
I walk under the moon
She has been my lamp
When I was restless in the night
When the jungle crept on claws or hoofs
Looking for a meal...
She was a searchlight
When I escaped the prisons
Or searched for the king n queen
Who fled with the royal family
Even upon the bed of love
The moon was a silver cover
To dreamy eyes who plucked stars
For bouquets of flowers
n toasted the sun with a full moon

I am one-thousand, nine-hundred & seventy-five years old
An encyclopedia of attitudes, feelings n ideas
Pounding in arteries n coronary-chambers of my heart
Flashing signals to my brain n senses
When I bleed
An entire river of history splashes gleaming
The blood spatters tell the stories of empires n conquest
If I piss there the flow of history
Speaks of lives untold in the backwoods
Of nations at the top, bottom n center of the world
Sun islands at mid-sea
The splashing of the toilet water
Are the shouts of jubilee
Of one great exclamation of humanity
I did live! I did go!
Even the dog by the fire hydrant
Sees the flow of animal history
Barking all the way down the sides
Of the fireman's leg
I am one-thousand, nine-hundred & seventy-five years old
I cry out in my opera voice
In bass to soprano
From slave-quarter to blue-stock blood
I am the horse
Who watered at the holes for centuries
Galloped when frightened
Attacked when angry
Offered horsemeat
Inside the jaws of a tiger
I am those jaws
Who enjoyed a blooddripping feast
Of pure raw flesh
It made me strong for the next kill
I pursued on the plains of india
or african bush
European forest
American mountain
...I am the great jaws
Who devoured all time

I am one-thousand, nine-hundred & seventy-five years old to be exact
As I register my time meter
Keeping exact count with the stars
By sun-tables n ancient astrologers
Or big ben in london
I must be correct!
The sweep of the hour
A ceaseless evening freeway
I must be correct!
A mad hatter
Of an albatross-clock
Chained round my neck
I must be correct!
In a minute or two
It will be one-thousand, nine-hundred & seventy-six
n I will have been assigned
By the president
To light fireworks
In the nest of eagles
n like a charming prince
I want to plant that kiss
Blowing the feathers off
The bald eagle
I must crack those eyes
The spell of evil charm
Has turned to nightmares
I must explode 1976
In firecrackers...
In firecrackers...
In firecrackers...
Wake up!
Wake up!
Its one-thousand, nine-hundred & seventy-six!
I say in my best impersonation of paul revere
Sounding like pancho villa
Doing wallace berry
I join a squadron of eagles
n collide with B-52s
Protecting the world
I fall back in a thousand shreds
Of u.s. savings bonds
I'm glued back together
In the laboratories of the c.i.a.
I am ready to take my place
In intensive care

In the same lungmachine
The eagles share
I am still lighting
Cherry bombs
Disguised as rosary beads of my age
Because regardless
Of one-thousand, nine-hundred & seventy-six years
I think it must be getting better
Even without the holy sermon
Of a norman v. peale
But...just because
I am still here...
You can catch me lighting fuses
Just about most any day
In the year
Of one-thousand, nine-hundred & seventy-six...
HAPPY BIRTHDAY AMERICA .

POET'S PRAYER PARA YUKIO MISHIMA

Valiant hot eastern bull
Bird of small feathers
Of large beak
You
Warrior of the red sun of japan
Were a dragon of fire
A whetstone to your knife
You sharpen everyday
In reverence to the tao
To the standing priest of time
Too slow in his prayer
His words like snails
That crawl the seas
So slow the priest of time
n you a warrior of lightning
With shoes of mercury
In the shinto temple
Cursing the universe
Where eagles fly
To the sun n back
You in your dark dream
Contrived revenge

Building monsters
To curse the priest of time
In prayer wheels
Or karate dance
You poured the sweat
From your heart
Until the coil
Reached the critical mass
Of hiroshima anger
n you grabbed the world
By the collar
n shouted of uprising
To the great island kingdom
n the priest of time
Smiled benignly
Folding inward great hands
In the chilly flapping wings
Of a nighthawk
n you were no more
As you lay silent
In the arms of hari-kari
Cursing the priest of time
Opening a galactic robe
Exposing the nine planets
Of our sun
For all to see the greatness
The wisdom
Opening n closing
In the revolving doors
Of life, death n universe
Or in the blossom of the cherry
Gathered by the winds
For utter dispersal
Smile priest of time
Fold us into your hands of prayer
For we walk on your tongue
On words from your stomach
In buckets from the well
We draw up your wisdom
We splash them upon the world
Cool grapes for the fire
At the very least

Good wine for the night
Of silver slippers
Hanging in wait
For strange feet
To walk upon the water
Great priest of time
I worship the east
A million times in one second
In a cavity of your tooth
O great one
We stand
In your legs
Asking for shoes
O great priest of time
Your eucharist
I will use
As a coin
For the pay-toilet
Or pay-phone
O great priest of time
Open your folded hands
That we may fly
As butterflies
n sing the song
Of canaries

STREET ICONOCLASTS

Am I crazy
With a tatoo on my arm
ESTA VIDA LOCA
A real don't give a good god damn emblem
In blue/red ink skin deep
Is this my badge
Does my generation speak thru me
The lower class of the inner city
The defiant/bad boy syndrome
The cruising short lookin' for the party-light-type

The attitude of my peers
Decorating their bodies
With symbols
Colorful like butterflies
Sometimes heavy rocks
To throw at people
Is the spirit
Of my reckless defiance
Any more unusual
Than two strange lives
By chance occurrence
Come together
In a strange light
Blinding with love
Worshipping at the local
Church of god
The real estate man
With plenty property
Is this maturity
Of the tatoo people...
Grown to long hair
And the love of good dope
And a reluctant understanding
Ain't supposed to die a natural death
But feeling cheated of life
That it should be otherwise
In the cause of the rebellion
That started with tatoos
I mean
What are we to do
We the tatoo people
With police priors
Of joining life
Breathing around us
The breaking of law
A thrilling encounter
I want to know why
Has this I.D. card
Been given me

I am beginning to think
I am of another world
An alien
Like my registration card
An immigrant
To the planet earth
By some great computer
Giving me permission
To live
I have not stopped counting the breaths
Of my thank you's
Beginning with my first one
And must I really be responsible
To your red, white and blue
There are so many other colors
To the rainbow spectrum
Must I be satisfied
With just one
The family of the rich
Have many colorful kingdoms
Must I really just have one
By birth mine is to the land of volcanoes
By life to the great bay of california
By wisdom to the planet
3rd from the sun
By circumstances to a condemned criminal
By imagination to a world
Whose umbilical cord
I have been cutting
With the creature
Who tatooed me

FEMALE FEMININITY

I stepped into the elevator
A perfumed smell overwhelmed me
Two women visitors
Touring the hospital
Left a business card
Of heavy aromas
I sniffed
And thought of the warm oyster
I have been a pearl to
I thought of woman
Flesh visions
Raced across my mind
In tunnel fantasies
In a mysteryhouse of beds
A funhouse of love
Sex hanging on the chandeliers
I thought of a coachman
Putting me in a pumpkin
Whisked away
In cadillac comfort
To a softly pillow
Of a woman's belly
My tongue swirling
In seagull dances
Above the sea of fish
My mind danced
In every corner
And private area
Of this encounter
Leaving a calling card
In the elevator
Now empty
Cold steel
And I alone
Descended to a world
Of tough faced men
On the lst floor
From the clouds
Of perfumed fantasies
Unmistakably
Woman

Unmistakably
I rode
The elevator
Alone
Into the void
Of sterile voyages
A eunuch
An appendage of the state
A sexless state
A loveless state
A merciless state
Who loves football
An a sixpack
With no time
For poetry
Or the possibilities
Of who you are
Or what
You mean
A swashbuckling
Brawling
Beerdrinking
Poetless
Loveless
State
I ride the elevator
Descending
To no
Nowhere...
Left with
A cloud
Of possibilities
Yet descending
To
Nowhere...

Mei Berssenbrugge

I was born in Peking in 1947. My mother is Chinese. My father is an American of Dutch descent. I grew up in Berkeley, California and then in Framingham, Massachusetts, so English is my main language. Though I've always written, I first studied it at Reed College and later at Columbia University. Since then I've traveled a lot and completed one book. I live in the small town of El Rito in northern New Mexico, in an old adobe house. The land here shows its history by color and shape but is still mysterious.

I'm glad to be a little part of the 3W pie. The writing, humane and energetic, means everything to me. Ideally rocks and bugs and corn and planets, etc., are one thing. My great-grandmother, a buddhist, used to buy fish at the market and set them free in the river, which was not practical.

I think writing is a way of making reality. Running makes the heart big. Making metaphors for what is real to us now, the same thing that science does, and shivering with what will be real. And I think it is collective work.

POOR MOUSE

We took the mouse alive
from the trap
and washed his cheek
and set him under some leaves
with a chicken bone by Ordway's gate
In the morning we found him crushed flat
by some heavy thing

When small creatures die
we are not to feel for them
They flow down into the river
and the ones crazed find a way
to live again

according to the weather
the horsetails and the wind:
in the cakepan
in the woodshed
in the hemlock trees
I hear a vibration fading away
but I never hear the thing striking.

BOOK OF THE DEAD, PRAYERS 14

Good-bye
try to stay awake now you're dead
and look hard at those demons
and don't be afraid.
All the bright lights and bells
are yourself returning
from wandering.
Try to look at them.
What terrifies
you must be beautiful.
I won't cry, make you sad.
If you embrace these assaults you'll be free.
But of course you are frightened.
Hair stiffens all over you.
So you'll fall
back down to us, back

into another dying body.
So I'll see you again.
Maybe without knowing you,
also knowing.
I tell you so you won't worry.
Try to stay awake.

TRACKS

Ond day you trip and jar yourself
and look around – all your friends
take out their false teeth
and offer them
yellow as old elephant bones

You touch your jaw
you can't tell
what animal shape you are
your spine curls
eyes grow shy
ears lengthen toward a muttering
you can't understand

There's a confusion of tracks
your nostrils catch
something recent
in the middle of an empty space
in the evening wind

Snout   hooves   a shining pelt
you set out in the blue air
remembering a horse you loved
as a child pressing its nose
against your plaid shirt

Try to remember now
what is a child?

FISH AND SWIMMERS AND LONELY BIRDS SWEEP PAST US

Today I love you so much I mistrust you -
our future bows out and swells
like liquid and falls under a bird's wing

each day runs after the other days
joining them with its tiny body
and heartbeats

Our bodies
lean toward center when we walk
sealed in a floating bell
phosphorus lighting up our eyes

and the bell is ringing
fish and swimmers
and lonely birds sweep by all around us

- and I look at you and you're invisible

EL BOSCO

(for Hieronymous Bosch)

If you offer your bag of butterflies,
seek honey, talk with a lion's head,
if you push fruit like a reptile up the mountain,
eat sprigs of rue from the cock's tail,
weep on your knees by the swan trail
like an angel or a goatherd,
if you cower in your crooked shack, awaiting
the small cherry-colored birds,
if you mourn,
despise skulls,
beat sinners like beggars,
hide manuscripts in the hollow of your foot
you'll still die;
even if you scathed your face with earthly jagged light,
even if you swept a little home for yourself
in a broken jug.

Joseph Bruchac

I live in Greenfield Center, a town in upstate New York in the foothills of the Adirondacks. The house I live in is the same one my grandfather built and as I grow older my connection to the soil grows stronger. The more you know of your roots, the more likely it will be that those roots will be strong, your life will bear fruit.

I run a college program in a maximum security prison (for Skidmore College), just finished a Ph.D. -- in Third World Literature and Creative Writing -- with the Union Graduate School, and have had 4 books of poetry published, the most recent of which is called *Flow,* from Cold Mountain Press.

More and more I look for the circle in my life and my writing... and in that circle I find the meaning of my own mixed ancestry, Slovak, English, Native American, and words which I can give to my own children.

THE DEER IN THE PRISON

One year a deer ran through the prison gate,
a white-tail buck the dogs had chased.
It swam across the Champlain Canal,
then ran along the fence until
it came to the place men were brought in
and turned there for a haven.

Some of those who were locked inside
saw it run across the lawns kept neat
by crews of cons with short bids left.

Was it killed or caught?
The man at the gate forgot.

Perhaps its ghost is running still,
running wild as these Northern hills,
running through some forgotten inmate's heart.

THE PATH

Half way between breath and Earth
colors borrowed from the Sky
the bent back of the Snake
above the gateway

in the shadow of the steamship's funnel
he watches
as three birds
fly beneath the arching path

the first is a bird of metal
its voice tears the air
the white chalkline of its passing
is too straight to form a circle

the second is a bird of flesh
it dips close in the wave
picks up a discarded orange peel
turns its wings into a window
of distance, flies through it, is gone

the third is the one which cannot be seen
its feathers brush his cheek

it is the one
he has returned to follow

/For Kofi Awoonor

BLACK SWEEPER

Paris/ 1974

In a faded grey suit coat
and blue bowler hat
he swishes his broom
of long brown twigs
across the sidewalk
and into the gutter.

His dark face
seems composed
though Haiti
and Dahomey show
in his astonished eyes,
as he turns, sweeps,
dips to keep
the water flowing,
turns and sweeps
papers and garbage
into the stream
which flows
to the sewers, the Seine
and the sea....

And as I walk
where he has passed
I see ahead of me
on grey pavement
moist half circles
and swirling designs
like the torn petals
of fallen dark flowers.

SNAKE HILL

Beyond the bumper cars
of Kaydeross Amusement Park
the hill rises two miles away
at the edge of Saratoga Lake
the great green head of an Earth snake

a hermit lived there
in the days when horses
followed the dirt road
at the water's edge
he made his living
from the bounty paid on rattlesnakes

each month at the County Seat
he brought in bags
filled with clicking rings
cut from the tails of arrow-headed rattlers

he had Indian blood
some people said
and wondered how
he found so many every year
every year and if
the words he used as
he stepped among the rocks
were the same as those we spoke

when he died
and people went to get
his few possessions
from his shack
they found in back
two dozen cages filled
with fat and drowsing tailless rattlesnakes.

CROSS FOX

Band of black across his shoulders
band of black along his back
the only stranger born into a litter
of red brothers and sisters
eyes bright, but his brighter
with another knowledge.

This is the one the breeders sought
the one whose blood would have brought forth
in the Fur Farm cages a rainbow of colors,
platinum, silver, costly gold.
This is the fox who was not caught.

The cross he carries on his back
is the four directions of this land,
the ways the People of the Dawn knew,
ways of the four winds and not the figure
held in carved agony, the dying god.

Living, he carries his cross
from the Earth
he was born in
back to the Earth.
He will not die in the air.

Americo Casiano

Poet and activist, born in Cabo Rojo, Puerto Rico, raised in the South Bronx and presently living there. Published in the *Greenfield Review, Latin New York* and *Revista.*

My poems have been in one anthology, *Neorican Poetry* from William Morrow and a book of my poems is forthcoming from the Greenfield Review Press in 1976.

I won a New York State CAPS grant in 1974 and the David P. Whiteside Award for poetry at Brooklyn College, where I've taught.

My poems are written from a socio-historic point of view.

PARA JUACO

(a message in two languages broken into each other)

;los ojos te miran!
entiende mi hermano.

;los ojos te miran!

como las aguas naturales del río de harlem / harlem river
ellos hablan un poema del sol
y companero,
usted es el sol
y el sol es un poema

pero te digo hermano
los ojos te miran!

you a vibrating tumbao in an ivy league suit
a cuatro por cuatro goin' wild
can you hear them / they play your song

pero brother-te lo digo otra vez
los ojos te miran

y qué del otro?
el llamado Maceo
I saw him
and i tell you man
los ojos te siguen mirando

Joaquín, Maceo mateo
bata - unanguá
the moon danced buffalo spirits in the nude
cause you a fine edged machete
like panther is your nickname
you wait to pounce on your prey
i tell you brother
los ojos te miran

como los traffic lights miran al antillano
de nueva york
empujándole agujas en los brasos arrebatados
y al mismo tiempe pintándose la cara

the room filled with jealous vibrations
brooklyn college gave a bulletin
General information;
aquí tienes dos panitas
La Viera Casiano
Casianola Viera
dos puños del Caribe
Casiano El Mar
La Viera La Tierra
juntos en las yoístas
apoyan tu posición
pues y qué de los ojos?
los ojos blancos / llamados riot squad
los ojos que se guillan de ser blancos / llamados chota!
si a esos ojos
que tiran balas de racismo
bochinches
y elloísmos

y que matan niños de 16 años
a esos ojos
yosotros de diremos
que el verdadero puertoriqueño
; es pura flama!

WE TALKED
(For M. Harper)

june first we spoke
and listened.

you spoke - i listened
you spoke - black - i listened
black - i heard - black - you spoke

i spoke - you heard
i spoke - brown - you heard
brown - you heard - brown - i spoke

we spoke - we learned
bed-sty - el barrio - we spoke
both the same
A Love Supreme.
A Love Supreme.

THE MUSIC BOX SANG

i arrived in mani
(translation peanuts)
driving thru Mayaguez
movement slowed
guanos lined streets
nodding in all directions
the music box sang

mama guela
mama guela

here stands acuario
bringing rains to mountains to coffee
Lares is green, brown,
a little salsa
fitting so naturally

mama guela
mama guela

coros of sea
make you lay iron on ground
shame on those who deny their browness

mama guela
mama guela

island rican lays in the cut
waiting to swing his machete freely
night came
we drank two bars
mama guela
mama guela

el coqui continues to sing

i will always eulogize those
mired in earth brown spirits
don't worry if you are defined by the sun
i'll give you key
just lay low
fake purr

standing alone / in a corner
i heard you.
you sang of a bird living / dead
and i remembered on a rooftop
one afternoon
a brother laid still
in a pool of urine
alone
eyes closed
sailing back.

(For M. Harper)

Melvin Dixon

Melvin Dixon has studied with Michael Harper and written plays while living in Providence, Rhode Island. His poems have appeared in numerous publications, including *Black World, The Greenfield Review*, and his poem "Climbing Montmarte" appeared as Broadside no. 86 in the Broadside Press Series. He has recently returned from an extended stay in Paris where the projects he was working on included a collection of poems called *God In Exile*.

SOUVENIRS

As I watch you leave again
I begin to measure my history in lines of old flesh
grown solid like the bark of trees;

I draw water from the beaten earth
and drain my blood into vials of porcelain
for tomorrow. Cold has seeped into this skin
from many more tears
than these . . . but I search
and I burn without ashes to search again.

MAN HOLDING BOY IN THE RAIN

Hunched forward under rain,
with his boy asleep in dungarees
locked to his chest, and pushing
against the steeled rhyme
of rain licking the skin
and bouncing from the beaded flesh,

He weighs this storm with eyes
no longer begging clouds for comfort,
but testing the ground
and the boy safe in his shoulders
rounded strong.

Rain spikes beating the old head
silence
once the boy awakes
and there are no more songs but his stirring.

THE SECRET OF SEEDS

Bulleted Red is dead, now
look for other mountaintops to bleed.
Langston's river floods this ground
leaving seeds dried in riversoil
seeds dried in dreams

listening for the Obeah man, yeah
listening for the Obeah man
Obeah, Obeah

Bulleted Red is dead.
Water no longer can tell the time of tortures.
This Dismal Swamp, her ochre leaves
salute the gods in exile,
having dried their seeds in riversoil
seeds dried from dreaming

listening for the Obeah man
Obeah, Obeah

Erzilie come Tuesday
Ogun this Friday noon and
set to fire Martin's madness
from yesteryears in riversoil of
ancient negro rivers as seeds

listening for the Obeah man
Obeah, Obeah

And heard beneath the rat worn stoop
the trance of voodoo mysteries a dance
and gods returning rush and rock the ages
in Obeah blues from gods in exile that
move the thunder and the light
back to the frozen hole of their swift exit,
Obeah, Obeah

seeds grown from riversoil
seeds grown from dreaming

FLIGHT ON NAKED WINGS

The wind as elder brother
calls to my red ribbed back
and I run

cold breath at the neck
chills my escape, my steps
sink in shadows
beneath the sun, the wind
calls me back to the bloodspot field
where death dispersed from
angry dandelion fluff
sharpens the grass
that scratches my skeleton feet.

Wind pulls me up from the ground.
The elder wind, my brother,
whistles through this skull
bone white from brown
and calls me home, pulling,
from bloodspots running.

Sandra Maria Esteves

The spring brings forth new life. In the image and spirit of woman, I, the center of all center, emerge as singing emerald of many-colored man. In the midst of agony and repression, of starvation and injustice, of transitory illusion and rightful reclamation, rises the voice of the multitude to become the ink which fills my pen. What matters the credits I could accuse myself. What matters the past which blew this sparkle through a door in the Bronx butcher shop of Lincoln Hospital, past the Taino Chieftains whose bones lay murdered over the hills of Utuado, Rio Piedras, Mayaguez, Lares, Jayuya, or the ship which transferred my father's father from island to mainland. Now come the message-bearers, whose past is the blood to twelve billion planetary slaves, whose present is a shopping cart full of ajax,
whose future?...well,

WE

determine.
Que Viva La Humanidad
Fuego y Espiritu
Free the Prisons

UNTITLED I-VIII

-i-

i am complexions of fire
degrees of burning coals
flavors of hot yellows and orange
tresses of molten rain
i create a breath
that warms the womb and penis
of birth
burning swift i sizzle thru
the breaking chills and plunge
to purify the cold stone, the new mountains
scorcher of eyes my tongue will bite
to melt away the tombstone
and shed a warmth to worms
and seeds.

-ii-

a cold place
detention house
not me
i'm glad not me
i said to him
inside
not me
i'm glad not me

but you are
said he
you are.

-iii-

when the snow falls softly
on faces
it caresses all parts
with the Love of a young mother

who is he
that would call the snow cold and ugly?

who is he
that would reject the breathing wind
carrying the spirit of life
perhaps, the soul of his next mother.

-iv-

the beginning
is a circle

the end
is
only words

die and
give life
to some worm
more humble
and productive
than you.

if you go one-way

you won't have to come back.

-v-

where is the tree on which i stand
and the sun around which i revolve
i search a sea
serene
a voyage
a soundless hour

-vi-

come into
a quiet warm
golden
in the middle of you

here
the place of eternity
the light
does not burn to touch

-vii-

For a sense of myself to sing
   what has been done and said
For a hope that has been flung from the west
   untouched with lines and shapes
Within the blades of one being
   the hearts of all being
Within the Voice of one child
   the Voice of the mountain
It is all prayer
To touch you aware that we
   are but one wind of thunder and breeze
We are but one rain that sprays the dew
   and rises mist of dawn
That we are the same of all names
And the music of all songs
That we are the pain of all disease
   cut and bled by our one sickness
And we are the cure the ray of light
The tropical bird that sparkles
   in shades of rainbow gem
The pearl shape of moon a solar form
Sound of no sound the womb
   a fire of stone the smell of sandalwood
The presence of life time the eternal flute
   panorama seashell sunset
The sweet earthly fragrance
   of maple oak and rose
All gathered in a slap of time
   a slow breath deep in a sense of myself
To sing what has been done and said again.

-viii-

i am the bird in transit for the winter
and the flame glowing, catching quickly

i am the dream that was lost within the wind
and the echo of a distant warrior's cry

i am the water flowing thru the rocky streams
and the bee sipping nectar from the blossoms

i am the noon sun reaching thru the trees
and the forming of the pearls within the sea

i am the noon sun reaching thru the trees
and the mountains standing proud against the wind

i am the harmony of the birds before the dawn
and the forming of the pearls within the sea

i am the space between the stars
and the shell around the snail

i am the eagle flying high
and the egg shaping life

i am the timeless
and spaceless

the burning
and freezing

the smallest
and greatest

i am love.

VANGAURDIA

they walk on the edge of the world
wage a war of peace
feed fires of creation
write the book of reality
nourish it
direct the wind of nations
disect the hate monger
pull apart the tentacles
with a prick of blood and intention
slowly building a fortress
soul upon soul
cement of sweat
sleepless dreamers
daggers of birth
they come in waves
of songs in pain
in fields of strengths
and growing stalks of thunder
they come from wet wombs
totally pushing the walls
of empty existence
breaking the fabric and crust
of rotting by-products

they come with faithful love
yearning to touch a deepless place
seeking a point of truth
that loves the universe
and sheds tears of joy
for the dawn that only rises
in the heart of unity.

UNTITLED X

i am poetry
waves of ocean
i dance
i am thunderstorm
dew and sea breeze
i am poetry
brown rice and spicy beans
the guts of mountains bursting
in volcanic song i am poetry
drum
conga beating thru the bloodstream
of my night and day
my valleys and hills
my wide moonlit plains i am poetry

i am you eyes of questions and answers
pregnant with desire and hunger

eyes of wisdom and sincerity
aged with the crust of years
of blizzards of silken webbed dreams
of stolen heritage and raped beauty

eyes of innocence and sunshine
playing forever in melodies of color

eyes of eastern horizons
the speakers of truth
i am you
farmer sculptor of earth wind and rain
warrior teacher child-bearer seed-sower
caught dead center in a mixture of sounds
revolving slowly
around the universe.

i am poetry.

Phillip William George

Phillip William George, after two years in Vietnam and a long year on the California desert as an Army dental technician, is now a freshman at Ganzaga University. He is a member of the Nez Perce Nation at Lapwai, Washington.

He spent much of his early life with his maternal great-grandmother, living and learning the ways of his ancestors. He arrived at the Institute of American Indian Arts in the fall of 1964, a graduate of Coulee Dam High School. He was a well-known traditional Indian dance champion of the Pacific Northwest. His art interests were in traditional costuming, music, dance, and writing.

Phil and the dance club of which he was president performed before national and international dignitaries in Washington. His poetry was read before Congress and translated into many languages for use on the Voice of America broadcasts. His poetry and prose have been widely published by educational and trade publishers.

After Phil's eighth birthday, his "real" name, given him at birth by his great-grandmother, was officially bestowed with feasts and ceremonies. Relatives and friends attended from the Colville, Spokane, Yakima, Warm Springs, Umatilla, Flathead, and Rocky Boy reservations.

Lah-peh-ya-low-ett, the name of his great-grandfather, refers to two white swans gliding above still waters, symbolic of beauty, grace, purity, and peace. At the naming ceremony, Phil's grandfather Seth explained the history of his father's sacred name.

"Lahpehyalowett lived across from the Palouse grasslands, east from the Kamiah valley. *Kamiah-pa* means 'the green valley with clear waters flowing through.' Lewis and Clark named the river Clearwater. The prairie adjoining pine forests allotted to Lahpehyalowett was perfect for horse raising. Because Lahpehyalowett owned hundreds of Appaloosa horses, the agent at Fort Lapwai named him Phillip, which means in Greek 'lover of horses.' "

AMERICA'S WOUNDED KNEE

First full moon of overgrown buffalo
Grass; missionary, settler, squatter.
Progress, they call it - they call it progress.
"Your past is best forgotten," says McGovern.
Justified genocide, not manslaughter,
and Medicine Man Crow Dog is imprisoned.
Trials begun with no Injuns on jury.

For seventy-one days the tepee stood,
Their solitary lodge, beside the church.
One more remains - just one percent left.

SPRUCE

assignment: death/education

She planted each spruce, blue as the Blue Mountains
From where they came.
Laden with child in womb, on horseback she went,
Bareback and alone.
Her floral-beaded saddlebags with fringe to hooves
Were filled with the last salmon run - smoked, sweet -
And the freshest of broiled venison and dried huckleberries.

In our little Switzerland, private and, "undiscovered,"
She made an opening in the forest:
She sang in the Sun where she uprooted a tree.
She planted each spruce - one for each child -
Seven healthy trees, strong in a row.
Except one.
That was Uncle in Korea.
She knew the second he was wounded when she
Detected yellow fungus on the bleeding bark.
Under Uncle's arms she slept until the telegram came.

In mourning she cut off her braids;
She planted them under the fungus - it disappeared.
She planted the telegram under his roots
Just like she planted salmon in the hole she
Dug with deer antlers when she planted each spruce.
Salmon returns to its same spawning stream
To die.

Anthropologists study "spruce worship"
And wonder . . . "Why?"
Sophisticated vultures in the shade of her spruce
Eating their lunch after picking our bones
And pulling her braids . . . laughing.

And I wonder: Why?

NAME GIVEAWAY

That teacher gave me a new name . . . again.
She never even had a feast, or, giveaway!

Still I do not know what "George" means,
    and now she calls me: "Phillip."

TWO SWANS ASCENDING FROM STILL WATERS must be
    too hard for her to remember -

SUNFLOWER MOCCASINS

Spring, and a new pair of moccasins!
These: floral beaded,
    with a sky-blue, Happiness background.

Now, I must race through
    Buttercup meadows to the timberline
    And bring a bouquet of
Flowers of the Sun to
Grandmother for celery.

When leaves and flowers change their colors
    She changes my moccasins
    as she pleases.

FAVORITE GRANDSON BRAID

I do not think Grandmother or Grandfather
    had a favorite grandson.

But still, with special care I weave
    three long strands above my left temple.

Their braid touches my heart.

MOON OF HUCKLEBERRIES

Black Bear sang, drumming on a log:
"Come, bring your biggest baskets
To the best berry patches -
    I'll show you."

"If you maidens get lost -
Just follow my dung. Just follow my dung."
Black Bear sang, drumming on a log.

WARDANCE

When you wardance, sometimes you must
Move like a bird - disguised in eagle feathers
    and secret fetishes.

And your enemies will fear
    This medicine movement of time and space -

Especially converted Indians allied with Longknives
    They are really scared!

TRUE:

(Insect of the Sun
    and of Happiness
Fluttered over me
    while I finished this poem:
A yellow butterfly.)

EAGLE FEATHER IV

Look up!
The Spirit is alive:
Ermine spots are clouds;
Sun streamers are horse hair strands
And the red and yellow is for New Days.

Look Up!
Eagle is of Freedom:
Gliding among clouds . . .
Catching light of the Sun . . .
Beginning our Tomorrows . . .

Look up.

SPOKANE FALLS 1874

Her veins incised - jagged boulders -
Earth's entrails tossed about -
Choice stones stolen to build
A 'chapel', they called it.

Vermin anglos have murdered their jesus
And now they have come to kill our Gods.

Palms calloused, or raw to bones,
Our backs humped from lifting, lifting,
With sorrow eyes, our heads were high.
Sun Father shines: Our shadows are ours.

Whipped! punished, or shot running if we
Dared to defy those black-robed priests.

Thunder and Waters went raging mad!
Vomiting white venom in floods - drowning
That cold, vile coffin of hypocrisy.
Our River Shrine was almost altered,
But, what a waste of rocks
For that, 'chapel,' they called it.

PRELUDE TO MEMORIAL SONG

100 Years Later

Dedication:

Descendants of the War of 1877
Chief Joseph Band of Nex Perce
Collville Reservation, Washington State

Before an audible sound, an almost recognizable
Tune: a puppy cry - a whimper from my heart.
Withheld burst of air pierces morning stillness.
An age old song follows the stream to Water's birth -
Up, up misty Nespelem Cascades where
Eagles and Salmon dance on rainbows.

Tears dry, I sing.
Steam rises from Owhi Lake and I sing.
For Long Time Age freedom I am lonely, so lonely.
amerika's whiteman's life makes me sad.
Am I alone?
Grandfather is dead.
Grandmother is dead.

Inside I bleed.
  I hurt.
  I hurt.
  I hurt.
Their song, a spirit portage,
Traces the spring to the mountainside.
With morning vapors my heart will rise
When red and yellow plumes go down between pines
My heart will rise.

I am alive.
Nemipu are Breathing Humans:
  We
      Are
          Alive.

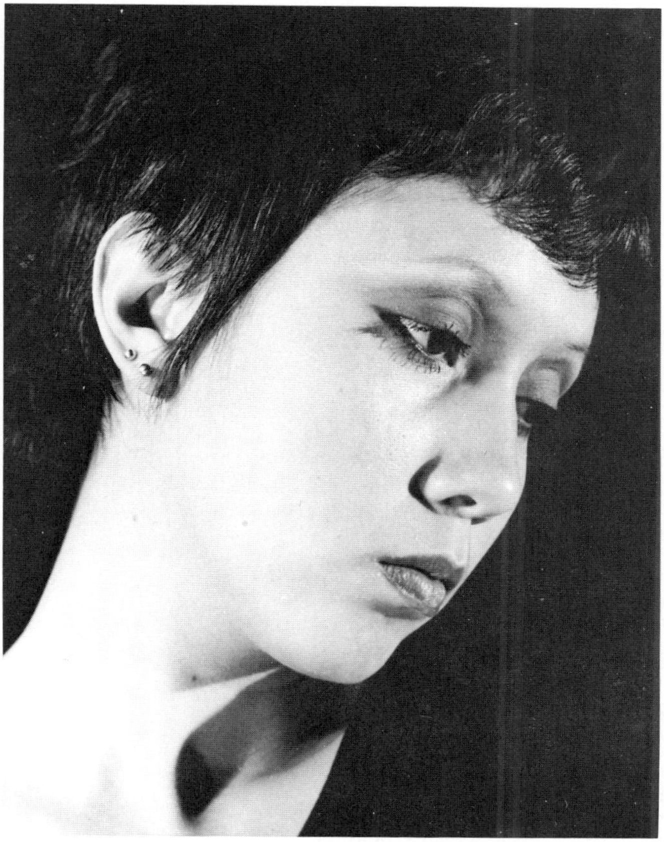

Jessica Tarahata Hagedorn

Jessica Tarahata Hagedorn was born in Manila, Philippines twenty-six years ago. She has published in four women's anthologies (*Third World Women, Four Young Women, Mountain Moving Day, Peace & Pieces*). A collection of her poetry (*Dangerous Music: The Work of Jessica Hagedorn*, Momo's Press), edited by Stephen Vincent, appeared in 1975.

SONG FOR MY FATHER

i arrive
in the unbearable heat
the sun's stillness
stretching across
the land's silence
people staring out
from airport cages
thousands of miles later
and i have not yet understood
my obsession to return

and twelve years
is fast
inside my brain
exploding like tears
i could show you
but you already know.

you greet me
and i see
it is you
you all the time
pulling me back
towards this space

letters are the memory
i carry with me
the unspoken name
of you,
my father

in new york
they ask me
if i'm puerto rican
and do i live in queens?
i listen to pop stations chant
to iemaja
convinced i'm really brazilian
and you a riverboat gambler
shooting dice in macao
during the war

roaches fly around us
like bats in twilight
and barry white grunts
in fashionable discotheques
setting the pace
for guerrillas to grind

the president's wife
has a fondness for concert pianists
and gossip
is integral to conversation

if you eat enough papaya
your sex drive diminishes
lorenza paints my nails blue
and we giggle at the dinner table
aunts and whores
brothers and homosexuals
a contessa with chinese eyes
and an uncle cranky with loneliness
he carries an american passport
like me

and here we are
cathedrals in our thighs
banana trees for breasts
and history all mixed up
saxophones in our voices
when we scream
the love of rhythms
inherent
when we dance

they can latin here
and shoot you
for the wrong glance
eyes that kill
eyes that kill

dope dealers are executed
in public
and senators go mad
in prison camps
the nightclubs are burning
with indifference
curfew drawing near
soldiers lurk in jeeps
of dawn warzones
as the president's daughter
boogies nostalgically
under the gaze
of sixteen smooth bodyguards
and decay is forever
even in the rage
of humorless revolutionaries

in hotel lobbies
we drink rum
testing each other's wit
snakes sometimes crawl
in our beds
but what can you do
in the heat
the laziness makes you love
so easily

you smile like buddha
urging me to swim with you
the water is clear
with corpses
of dragonflies and mosquitos
i'm writing different poems now
my dreams have become reptilian
and green
everything green
green and hot

eyes that kill
eyes that kill

women slither in and out
of barroom doorways
their tongues massage the terror
from your nightmares
the lizard hissing nervously
as he watches you breathe

i am trapped
by overripe mangoes
i am trapped
by the beautiful sadness of women
i am trapped
by priests and nuns
whispering my name
in confession boxes
i am trapped
by antiques and the music
of the future

and leaving you
again and again
for america
the loneliest of countries

my words change . . .
sometimes
i even forget english

CHRISTINA

1.
auburn is a chic color
not too much red
if you overdo it
you look like a whore

wheat
is the new shade
in clothing
wheat suede coats
wheat silk shirts
wheat gabardine pants
with matching luggage
and matching south american
tycoons
with cigars stuck in their mouths
to chauffeur you around
in mercedes-benz sedans

2.
older men
make better lovers
they know
how to treat you good
at all times
offering arabian stallions
and private helicopters
as homage
to your timelessness

this is the life
the movie is based on
where rita hayworth
changes her name
and loses twenty pounds

3.
never admitting
her love
my mother's anger
is her real strength
like an aging tigress
still beautiful
in the afternoon light

i could never tell her
how much i want to touch her
sometimes
fear runs deep
in her eyes
i can see it mingle
with her rage
the paranoia there

what could doctors tell me
that i haven't already guessed
the paranoia
that raised me
and cristina
with her wonderful breasts
stunning the world
in her saks fifth avenue
brassiere

4.
i've lost my appetite
for love
many times
but it's my mother
i still think of
as all women
a common occurrence
but still frightening
when i'm alone

5.
my mother
plays rita hayworth
in my dreams
and she dyes her hair
auburn

leaping
on cafe tables
and tempting men
with her fiery flamenco

in hollywood
some kind of ethnic mix-up
between mexico
and spain

ahh. . . . those latin lovers
they all sigh
but not true
not true

only the dagger
in her thigh
does not lie

CANTO DE NADA

her name is nada
daughter of ainu and t'boli
igorot and sioux
sister to inca and zulu

born from the mouth
of a tree
the lullaby
of joe loco and mongo
turquoise eye
the lullaby
of pattie labelle
and the bluebells
flowers of her smile
the strut   the style

she is the punk
the dancing girl
the brand new bag
purple and red
the brand new bag
the sweetness
the lullaby
of herself

the riff of a biwa
the daughter
of a sorceress
the gong
the dragon lady's baby

she is the punk
the dancing girl
la cucaracha
who can even get up
from her own o.d.
every night
the color of her hair

she is the song
soul sister number one
the brand new bag
her jewels are as loud
as her love

her name is nada
mother to rashid
koumiko carmen miranda
ylang-ylang ruby delicious

she is the cocaine princess
with the hundred dollar nose
getting higher
because she's got to aim
for the stars

she is the star
she is the city
flaunting sequins
and butterflies

she is peru mindanao
shanghai
the divine virgin
waiting for a trick
on the borderline
between emeryville
and oakland

at noon on sunday
at noon on monday
at noon
hail mary
full of grace

she is nada
all music
she is nothing
all music
she is the punk
all music
the dancing girl
all music
she is nada
nothing
she is the real thing
and in her womb
you could sleep

for days

SORCERY

there are some people i know
whose beauty is a crime.
who make you so crazy
you don't know
whether to throw yourself
at them
or kill them.
you better be on the lookout
for such circumstances.

stay away
from the night.
they most likely lurk
in corners of the room
where they think
they being inconspicuous
but they so beautiful
an aura
gives them away.

stay away
from the day.
they most likely
be walking down the street
trying to look ordinary
but they so fine
they break your heart
by making you dream
of other possibilities.

stay away
from crazy music.
they most likely be
creating it.
cuz when you're that beautiful
you can't help
putting it out there.
everyone knows
how dangerous
that can get.

stay away
from magic shows.
especially those
involving words.
words are very tricky things.
everyone knows
words the most common
instruments of illusion.

they most likely
be saying them.
breathing poems
so rhythmic
you can't help but dance.

and once
you start dancing
to words

you might
never stop.

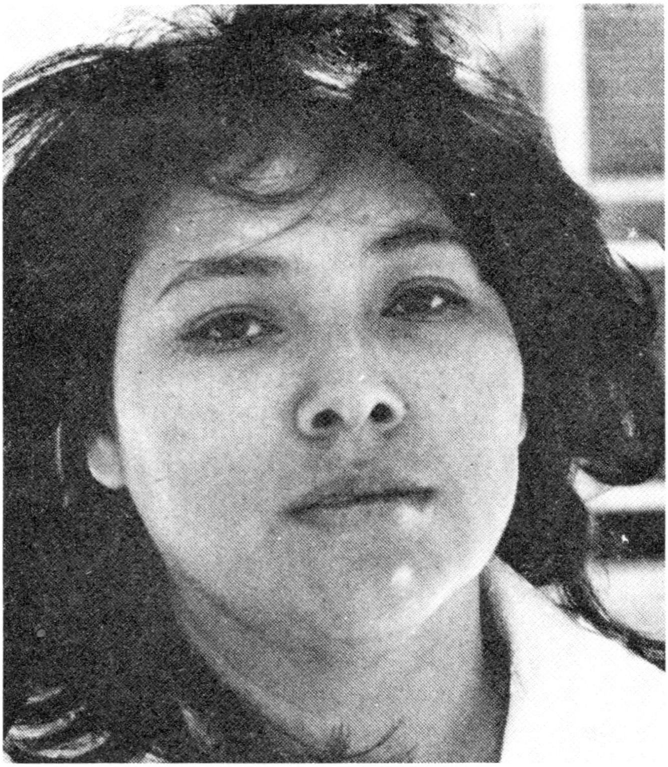

Janet Campbell Hale

"Writing for me has always been a means of imposing order on experience, making sense of things. I never graduated high school and I came from a poor family. I am a member of the Coeur d'Alene tribe of Northern Idaho and I was born and raised on the reservation. Times were very hard when I first came to the city. I wrote poetry, stories, essays because of a deep personal need."

Janet Campbell Hale studied law at the University of California at Berkeley. She has published in several anthologies (*Whispering Wind,* Doubleday, 1970; *Third World Women,* Third World Press, 1972; *People of the Rainbow,* Viking, in press) and has written a novel (*The Owl's Song*).

ALLIGATOR BITES

A tiny scratch upon your
Chubb-sweet arm,
One of the kittens, I think,
Struggling to escape
Your smother-love,
Hugs and kisses,
Or your trying to wrap them
In old rags
And make babies of them,
One of them must have made
That hurt you hold up
For me to kiss,
"An alligator bit me," you say,
Like you always do,
Your big, brown eyes,
Reflecting sincerity,
"Whatever you say," I say,
Gladly kissing
Your hurt away.

MY SISTERS THE SUMMER OF 53

I hated the way my sisters looked,
With their hair in tight pincurls,
Getting all ready to go out.
"It shows the shapes of your heads,"
I'd tell them.
"So? What's wrong with that?"
They'd ask.
" Plenty," I'd say.
But oh, they'd look glamorous
Later on,
Curls, powder, lipstick,
Going to the dance or show
With some guy or another,
Some Indian cowboy type
(Sometimes they'd come courting
Carrying their guitars and sit outside,

Playing and singing:
Jumbolaya and a Crawfish Pie, or:
I picked her up in a Pickup Truck, or:
Hey, Hey, Hey, Good-lookin',
Wha' Wha' Wha'cha got cookin'.
How I envied them
Those balmy summer evenings,
When they were almost women,
And I was little yet.

TRIBAL CEMETARY

I lay my hand
Upon
The coldness of the smooth
White stone,
My fingers touch the words,
I read again:
My father's name,
Date of birth,
Date of death,
Veteran of
World War I.

"This is your
Grandfather's grave,"
I tell my children,
Wishing I could tell them,
That they would understand,
That the man
Who was my father,
Was of that first generation,
Born on old land
Newly made reservation,
That at twelve,
He went to Mission School,
To learn to wear shoes,
To eat with knife and fork,
To pray to the Catholic God,

To painfully
Learn English words,
English meanings,
White ways of thinking,
English words,
To speak,
To think,
To write,
English words,
When we,
My children
And me,
Know no others.

I lay my hand
Upon
The cold white
Stone,
My daughter,
Who is four,
Gathers small rocks,
With which she
Fills her pockets,
She sings to herself
As she goes along.

My son,
Who is ten,
Stays with me awhile,
Beside my father's grave,
Asks me about my
Childhood,
About the others
Lying buried here,
In Campbell-labeled
graves.

Then he leaves me,
And goes about
The cemetery,
Reading tombstones,
For unusual names,
Looking for people,
Who lived
One-hundred years,
Or more - -
He's found five.

Michael S. Harper

I was born at home (March 18) 1938, in Brooklyn, New York where I attended public schools; my parents moved the family to Los Angeles in 1951 and I attended high school and college before writing any poetry. I had written plays and short fiction for creative writing classes, worked as newspaper distributor, lifeguard, postal clerk, counselor, and in 1961 spent a bad year at the University of Iowa's Writers' Workshop, where I wrote fiction and poetry, sold pennants at football games, and read in the University library to avoid the cold. After some jobseeking I taught functional writing at LACC, then moved to San Francisco where I married and had a son, Roland (two others died shortly after birth). I began to publish poetry in journals in the late sixties and traveled to Mexico and Europe where those landscapes broadened my scope and interest in poetry and culture of other countries while I searched my own family and racial history for folklore, history and myth for themes that would give my writing the tradition and context where I could find my own voice. My travels made me look closely at the wealth of human materials in my own life, its ethnic richness, complexity of language and stylization, the tension between stated moral idealism and brutal historical realities, and I investigated the inner reality of those struggles to find the lyrical expression of their secrets in my own voice. After teaching in Portland, Oregon; Hayward, California and Urbana, Illinois, I presently teach and direct the writing program at Brown University, and live with my wife and three children in Rhode Island.

Publications: *Dear John, Dear Coltrane* (University of Pittsburgh Press, 1970); *History is Your Own Heartbeat* (University of Illinois Press, 1971); *History as Apple Tree* (San Francisco, Scarab Press, 1972); *Song: I Want a Witness* (University of Pittsburgh Press, 1972); *Debridement* (Doubleday, 1973; *Nightmare Begins Responsibility* (University of Illinois Press, 1975).

HEARTBLOW

"When a woman take the blues,
she tuck her head and cry.
But when a man catch the blues,
he grab his shoes and slide."

Near The White House

A cross is a machine
in a ship's hull,
an anchor on the Potomac
is a mansion.
This black statue curtseys
in a vanilla smile,
its lips a cross
burning, its heat
flicking the mansion lights:
beacons on the marbleheads
and a sorrow song is a cross.

Rat Fever: History As Hallucination

A man's a man
when he can kill
rats with bare hands,
eat them
or be eaten by them.

Tracked leavings
on the village roof,
out the window
sewers overflowing:
a man's a man
when he can eat himself up
and leave no tracks.

The Meaning Of Protest

Between the world and me
a black boy is a native
son with a long dream
if a white man will listen.
Uncle Tom's children
were eight men, all outsiders,
fishbellies living
underground.

Pagan Spain taught us the church
was woman as mystery, a penis
the sword to butcher each other;
Black Power! we're not going
to the moon, and in Bandung
white man can't come,
he's on a savage holiday.

Blossoms in a peanut field
won't bring me home;
something in the hum
of cotton is a glue
that won't hold red soil still;
ten million voices spliced
on an iron cross
between the world, and me, and you.

Parable

Black-stemmed ax
stuck in white tree;
roots in waterhole
roped underground
get tree fever;
cut off handle,
tree die.

History As Diabolical Maternalism

When I grind glass
I think of lenses
swallowed like sugar,
a preacher with glass eye,
a eunuch named Jesus,
Black Mary in his cottonfield.

Heartblow: Messages

I sit in cubbyhole,
wasp nests north and south,
woods to the west, ocean east,
the highway north a southern road
Goggle-eyed lamplights
blink uneven wattage
as the pulses
of your soulful heart.

I met a man who gave you bread
and meat and a warm bed
while you wrote BLACK BOY,
another who shared your Chicago loft;
some wait for released papaers,
some salve old photographs.

A campus librarian near
Hollywood reads the unread
books to move with Bigger,
sees Mary's spittle as sperm
pushing her trunk,
holds the body as you hack her neck,
watches Bessie's downdraft
as a cross-corner shot.

The parable of black man, white woman,
the man's penis slung to his shin,
erect, foaming in that woman's womb,
the ambivalent female with smirk-shriek,
daylights of coitus stuck together,

through the nights the razored solution;
that the black man is nature,
the woman, on her drilled pedestal, divine,
the man with razor an artisan
in symmetry steel and sharp blades -
let him melt into his vat of precious metal,
let the female wipe her face of sperm,
let the black man's penis shrink to normal
service, let the posse eat their whips instead.

On the Seine I thought of you
on the towpath to Notre Dame;
at the Blue Note looking for Bud
on his *parisian thorofare*;
caught your blues from black musicians
while you died alone in prose;
some said you'd died of disconnection;
souls said you dealt your own heartblow.

Spiritual

Grandma's picket fence
balloon mask dancing
bloody moon your black ribcage.

Afterword: A Film

Erect in the movies
with a new job,
Trader Horn
and *The Gay Woman*
unfold in a twinbill:
drums, wild dancing,
naked men, the silver
veils on the South Side.
He imagines nothing:
it is all before him,
born in a dream:
a gorilla broke loose
from his zoo
in a tuxedo; baboon.

You pick your red bottom.
The Daltons are the movies.
On my wall are pictures:
Jack Johnson, Joe Louis,
Harlow and Rogers:
"see the white god and die."

Underground I live in veils,
brick and cement,
the confession beaten out,
slung with hung carcasses,
a bloody cleaver grunting,
a dead baby in the sewer:
"all the people I saw were guilty."

Marked black I was shot,
double-conscious brother in the veil–
without an image of act or thought
double-conscious brother in the veil

The rape: "Mrs. Dalton, it's me,
Bigger, I've brought Miss Dalton
home and she's drunk:"
to be the idea in these minds,
double-conscious brother in the veil–
father and leader where is my king,
veils of kingship will lead these folks
double-conscious brother in the veil–
"see the white gods and die"
double-conscious brother in the veil–

Lawson Fusao Inada

"Make your statement!"
-- Admiral George Takei, aboard the carrier Asian Enterprise

(GONG) My name is Rice Field, is what it means, is where I'm from: the Windward Side of Fresno, officially designated a Wilderness Area. Manning a station here in the Yukong Delta Region of Origami, I wear a Black Belt on ceremonious occasion, presiding as Most Likely.

As is customary, we test for depth by chanting "To-shi-ooo! Mo-riii!" and "Frrrank! Chinnn!" as one can fathom, though the local aboriginal 'ethuhniks' (corruption of epicanthic) can comprehend us only through our limited dispensation of their fortunes: "uh oh" & "If..." & "Keep Peking straight ahead, podner" & "That's the way the ol cookie..." etcetera. (Hopefully, through our dedicated efforts, the capacities of these unfortunates will be raised to functional levels.)

To commemorate our Multimillennial this Dynasty, selected emissaries rode rotary rickshaw roughshod over this remote and practically uninhabited (except for roving bands of "murkans" and voracious "senior citizens" -- to use their inscrutable pidgin) peninsula to Canton, Ohiogozaimasu, coastal outpost of The Shogunate -- where He quelled the invading southern barbarians and crushed and subjugated the northern dwarves -- stopping at Lan Sing for ten thousand supplies, then Ahn Ahbah for a solar ride aboard the mystical airwaves of Eminent Guru Rice Furrows before offering biodegradable seawater to the Six Winds high atop the steeps of Bowling Green, paying ritual homage to our Sacred Sage of Jade and Sport.

From His Honorable Mouth, and through the True Tongue of Poeters Phil George, Nez Perce Nation, and Clyde Kusatsu, East West Players, two ancient and recurring fables which I humbly convey to you, Gracious Reader:

1. Just about these entire pages did wilfully stride into one "Hot Fish Shoppe (sic)" in the colony of Stevens Point (Walleye Stevens, self-styled militant "acupuncturist", ill-fated founder of the aboriginal "mongoloid" cult of "insurance"), province of Hwes-Khan-Sing, intent upon discovering advancements, if any, in occidental cuisine (loosely applied, but preferable to "grub", which, nevertheless, is suitable to appearances). The local "ms-host-person" (such dire confusion of Confucian morality!), visibly impressed by their elegance and refined deportment, did correctly inquire -- "juhgot reservations" -- which they certainly had, and therein proudly replied: "Certainly. Two: Nez Perce and Laguna!"

2. Subsequently, crossing the "drag" in front of one "Poor Henry's" (predictably, these infidels have a childlike fascination for vulgar nomenclature, and no capacity for preparing fish), a "rig" (corruption of rickshaw) bearing all of "texas" (a malodorous concoction of "hah skewl futbawl"/native excrement, crucial to their perverse "revivals" and "klan (sic)" mythology) careened around a corner toward their ambulatory party. Graciously, they obliged its safety, stepping back upon the "gut-her", whereupon the "rigor" gratefully offered a quaintly primitive salute -- central digit lifted to His Highness The Sun. Bowing, they chanted in unison: "He is *always* Number One!" (GONG)

NAMELY YOU

"uh-one/uh-two/uh-here-we-go...." -- Sonny Rollins,
"Namely You", *Newk's Time*

could be Kelly
could be Watkins
could be me
could be you

sitting here in the dark
of my dead
grandmother's parched
reflection
with a need for the wet
of Wynton's fingers
the booming
deep that is Doug

pulling into that dead
spun vortex
or, the whirl
reversed, spraying us with
musical illumination

that death can do
that has no
shadow
but its own
illumination

where the pure
fluids
continually run
in all the illumined
colors we know we are

you know me
I moved among you
touching you
yellow
with all my
will to dance and sing

who, then
would have it other-
wise

even among space
less suffocation
or places
with so much
arid room
we can die
of internal erosion

the song is there
listen to it
the enduring dance
of strength and survival
that will have it
otherwise
now

these fools continue
to surprise me
not at all
laughing and dancing here
The Mad Jap of the Mountain
with voluptuous
does snapping their fingers
racoons crooning flutes

I am under waterfalls
whistling
dancing in the rapids
of roads

and those
who cannot hear me
who cannot ever find me
in continual rearview
violate the tracks of my dance
and call me
Big Foot
Nigger
Geronimo
Wetback
Chink

and set elaborate traps
because they do not want to
ever catch me
in the sleep of their wives
or in the waking
lives of their children
who have sense enough
to follow

tonight, in the blue
pool of the wise rock
of my living grandfather
looking out
to my grandmother's yama,

I let the darks of my eyes
illumine
spun strings
from here to there
from me to you
and back again
where I continually am

singing
left hand
gleaming Asian constellations
right hand
strumming all our
fragrant shades

dancing with continual
illuminations
between us

that are Wynton
that are Doug
that are, yes, you
Alex
that are Bruce
that are Frank
that are Gary
that are Javier
that are Joe
that are Leslie
that are Mbembe
that are Mei Mei
that are Melvin
that are Papo
that are Phil
that are Ricardo
that are Ron
that are Sandy
that are Sharon
that are Shawn
that are Suni

that are
ummmmmm hmmmmmmm
namely me

that are
you better believe it
people

namely you

AT THE STRONGHOLD

(For Miles and Toti)

Miles is so sufficient
he makes me
breakfast with a flick of his wrist --
little cakes
of oceans and islands.

Toti is into
stirring,
mostly,
but if I ask him
he picks the burrs
off the tops of my socks.

Then they demonstrate
the adaptability
of scissors and cardboard,
making up games
that rule about life.

I give them
many-bladed knives,
little men in blue diving suits

and remember me.

There's a cool
Tlingit wind
blowing over
water all the way from Japan
blurring the surface
of my eyes,
the deeps
pulling me
down and in.

\- - - - - -

Up over Greensprings,
the pass, crash
of wheeled
cataracts
screaming logjams
into and out of
switchbacks
with a flick of fins.
Eyes. Brown
eyes of bottles,
squirrels
that never learn.

- - - - - -

Count your
self
lucky
to find a deer
by Pinehurst. Bless
you.
She
is the soul
of women among huckleberries,
soft, fine eyes

before the invasion,
the cry.

- - - - - -

Lately, in the drought,
I am obsessed

by clouds, their
forming, knowing

them only as
dispersal flowing

over me
lately

in the drought.

- - - - - -

K Falls ain't
got nothing
for me.
Unless I had a need
for gutters, for

official termination,
my brown eyes
welling over at the rim

brown spit
bottoms of bottles,

my brown spirit
slumped in some stirrups

at the terminal.

- - - - - -

Hell, I'm not trying to do
nothing for nobody
but me,

my own cause,
my destiny

come round
to me.

I need my own
sense
shaped into place

in a strong body with
whole bones
with no

disease in the marrow,
the smolder of shrapnel.

Not even the need
for legend,
something

monumental to build on,
something
grand, just
my self,
my own scope and destiny,

so when my
time comes, I can go
off and die

like a man.

- - - - - -

Captain Jack,
I come to you

in respect,
out of a need

for communion.

I will not dance and sing
in your sacred cinders

where even today
the trail
is difficult to walk upon.

We, too,
walked upon this ground,
and though our
stronghold
was made for us,
to hold us in,

we, too,
heard the geese in the wind,
the wind in the tules

and dreamed
in our brown bodies

of peace and the good land,

of home.

\- - - - - -

And so I come to you,
Captain.

And if you were to meet me
on the difficult terrain
of a parking lot
you would extend your hand to mine.

\- - - - - -

There is a mystery
how you survived

this desperate place
of edges and wind.

The commissioners were many.
They bled in the heat.

There were so few of you.
What did you eat?

There is no mystery.
Fat white ladies with small dogs
and weak husbands
are still on the track.

The lava bed
is a place to sleep.
Heat, rain, cracked
sweet cinders, the red
tule rope of resistance -

this is how we sing and survive -

the entire
one of us
gorged with the knowledge

of paved genocide
trying to find its way here.

\- - - - - -

Here, in this stronghold
I have hid my heart,

a battlement
strong at the marrow,
stored there

for when the time allows,

fists in the throat,
a volley
of words and rocks
in strong
boxes

back of the heart
behind mazed
trails spiraling

to my music,
where no one is allowed.

Here, in this stronghold,
I hide
myself
to myself,

deaf with my pulse
running through the walls

where my life is carved,

ancient signs
where the hurts happened,
the loves, the births,

all in calligraphy
that nothing but the blood

deciphers,
or cares

to be allowed

to this stronghold

where I show my heart.

- - - - - -

"Question 27: Are you willing to serve in the armed forces of the United States, in combat duty, wherever ordered?"

No.

"Question 28: Will you swear unqualified allegiance to the United States of America and faithfully defend the United States from any and all attack by foreign or domestic forces, and foreswear any form of allegiance to the Japanese emperor, or any other foreign government, power, or organization?"

No.

Hirohito?
Him people
like you na me.
Me no go
Chinchinahtee.

Me go
Tule Lake.
Me stay
Carifonia.
Home.

\- - - - - -

All I wanted
was a place to live,

how we had always known,

women among huckleberries,
tules that teach
children of junipers, geese, and sky.

All I wanted
was to fight to live,
to be left alone.

All I wanted
was a concession to dignity,
our own reservation.

All I wanted
was our own
defeat.

All I wanted
was to die.

\- - - - - -

Looking into the eyes
                                        of my children,
                                        the gifted young

who wished me in women's clothes,
who silently called me
                                        white and compromiser,

I see the *why*

I am
the renegade
I am,
the revolutionary
I will always be.

What land we had
we must have back again.
This is the stronghold,
the heart, the spirit
in the land, the heart,

This termination, this
extermination, this
compromise to survive.

The fenced-in barracks
still stand
beyond the ancient carvings
of Prisoner Rock.

The signs are right.
The spirit. The land.
We must have back again.

Those of us still alive
singing assimilation
with the flick of wrists,
thrive on the sick
blood of subjugation
here on this very land
where we died.

Captain Jack
will be hanged
tomorrow. "Instructions
to all persons
of Japanese ancestry. . ."

This is the stronghold,
the heart, the molten
flow solidified
blood of ancestors.

The blood of us
is the red tule rope.

What are you worth
in the eyes
of your sons?

The blood of us
is the red tule rope.

- - - - - -

As our stay increases -
summer into fall -

the wounds and pain
fall from our feet

as we begin to know
the paths
of the stronghold
the scars of battle
smooth places
to stand upon

as our stay

increases
to the span
of our life

as we begin to see
buttes and geese,
juniper and sky

as all clouds
form at Shasta
and return there.

Captain Jack,
father,

you teach us

to stand
to plant
our feet in the ground

you teach us

to stand
to raise
our eyes from the ground.

- - - - - -

My sons,
you are beside me now.

No.
You will not be leaving
for Oklahoma.

No.
No one will take your photo
in front of barracks.

Yes.
We are willing to serve.

Yes.
We swear allegiance.

And if my old time is allowed,

I will go off into the hills

with the flute of my father

and sing the song

of geese in the wind

of wind among tules

of the red tule rope

of blood that always flows

of clouds around Shasta

and listen, and grow

silent and still

in my own, in my own

wisdom and dignity

as a man.

Karoniaktatie (Alex Jacobs)

My name is Karoniaktatie, meaning 'Where the Sky Meets the Earth'; it is a good name but not a turtle clan name, of which I am a member...in other words: i am a turtle...slow...intermittently thick and thin shelled...patient (??) supposedly but definitely a run of snapping turtle in me...

At this time (September '75), I am 22 and readying myself to head out west for a lengthy stay in Sante Fe, New Mexico at the Institute of American Indian Art; to learn from the many Native students, teachers and their peoples' ways; hopefully turn some people on in Mohawk-Iroquois-Northeast ways, not that they haven't been already as we are known for being wanderers/travelers/displaced and messengers of our own way.

I've spent a year at Manitou Community College in Ecowi, Quebec as a student and printer/graphic artist at the Thunderbird Press there. It is the only print shop of its kind run by and for Native peoples in Canada, perhaps North America, but surely not for long.

My interests are many...and would like to get my hands in more...writing poetry, editing poetry books, illustrating, carving, making clay pipes, masks & shields, painting, farming are what I've been up to...sculpture, music & dance, drama, are other media I want to be part of and in...

Poetry editor of *Akuesasne Notes* 1972-1974 and still a contributor. *Notes* published and distributed my work and prints on tapes, *Native Colors* being the first of my collections.

1,000,001 STARLINGS

& white folks freakin
as starlings & blackbirds
congrgate & talk things over
holding their Unity Conference

eat away every bit of food & leaf
& shit on anything left over
til it looks like a winter
thats never gonna end ...

& when the sun comes out
it smells like its Never gonna end

they're raising a stink, these birds

over these white folks freakin
its called a taste
a taste of your own medicine

SPIRITS/SOMEONE

. . . walk thru the house
they can be heard
looking over things
utensils
fondling remembrances

of ages   whispering   cooing
& other times
discarding modern tools
with a thump thud . . .

CALIFORNIA GOLD RUSH

california
gold rush
what a rush
thot u kilt all
de indins

no indins
no treedees

whatza treedee
nashun?
whatza indin
nashun?
whatza nashun dat
built its foundation
in blood mine/yours
Stick its stainless steel
supports in my belly
covers my eyes with
redwhite & blue lies
sucks my blood
& my sperm
dats amerika
dats amerikan nashun

california
gold rush
what a rush
indins make baskets
not war
indins collect roots & berries
not scalps

now
all de gold gone
but california keeps on
rushing
stick his dick into
de Rivers
want de power
e-lek-tris-i-tee
want de mtns
trees for toilet paper
yeah california
pg&e is de new rush
pg&e say "Pit River?"

whatzat
dis amerika
amerika need juice
to run its macho machines
sorry we thot u all dead
no treedees
no land
dis progress
we gonna Stick
right here

so blood flows
from conquistador lance
from colt 44
& long knife
thru pg&e transformers
blood flows like oil
on de ocean
california keeps on riding
to hawaii   phillipines
china   vietnam

california
gold rush
what a rush
u need Pit River
to wipe LA's ass
u need Alcatraz
to make tourist bucks
u need Maidu graves
for Reagans mansion
california
dats not a tan
dats my caked blood

what a rush

THERE'S A FOOTPRINT OF LOVE & DISORDER

theres a footprint
of love & disorder

a light handed touch
on the universal drum
local/secular drone
of bees and flutes & strings
voices rampage thru water
loves footprint on my pillow
loves footprint in the sand

a digger discovered
the goblet in the morning
atop a hoary mound of sand
& neath the white sand were
a crowd of footprints
once people, all pointed inward
in a forever sea of stone

when you dig in graves
be true to yourself someway
drink the blood & the dust
join the circle
amputate with shovel
any convenient appendage
& tell your children
to tell your grandchildren
not to worry or think
about your stinky ol bones

there was never any pain
to speak of . . .

("Daddy . . . kin we go see gram-
pas bones at the mooseum?")

DREAM SONGS

colours
painted on you
as rainbow
as morning

colours
painted
on you
as flowers

colours
i saw

in the mist
the trees standing
in the mist
the marsh listening
in the mist
eagle flew
in the mist
with wings of fire

the loon
breathing
dancing

into my eye
breathing
dancing

sing
    for me
the song
        the quiet one
when
    last we met

in
  deep water
your smiles
  come to me
i
 am
    drowning

TROLL SONGS

i am growing
Look! i am growing
    i am growing
    my moccasins
    i can't fit
    my leggings
    i can't fit
    my shirt
    i can't fit
    even my pouch
    the belt too small
    my gustoweh*
    it fell off

    my hair dances
    in the wind now

    naked
    i am growing

yes, only naked will i grow

**or kastoweh: old time iroquois hat*

like an eagle
i am
i am flying
i
can't fit my chair
      you want it?

feeling free
feeling free
squatting
arms folded
round my knees
how much like
a bee i feel
my eyes among
these flowers
feeling free
feeling free
i took a shit
really
      truly
            a wonderful load
                        unload
watch out
(if you're like that)

Geraldine Kudaka

Geraldine Kudaka has recently returned to the U.S. after a year's sojourn in Asia. Her poetry has appeared in the anthologies *Time To Greez* (Glide Publications) and *Japanese American Anthology* and is scheduled to appear in a forthcoming anthology from Houghton Mifflin, as well as having been published in such magazines as *The Greenfield Review* and *Heirs Magazine.*

One of her long poems, "Anatomy of a Continent" has been performed with a three piece band and a dancer. She is currently working as a CETA curator for the San Francisco Art Commission's new cultural centers and trying to complete a manuscript of short stories, while doing a column for a rock magazine on film. She is also part of a writer's collective, *Renga* (named after the Japanese form of poetry), which is working with *Heirs Magazine* on putting together a campaign related to the issue of housing.

Geraldine Kudaka's first book of poetry *Exiles And Passages Of Return* is scheduled for publication in 1978 by The Greenfield Review Press and plans are afoot for a simultaneous publication on cassette tape by *Black Box* of her reading her poetry with musical accompaniment.

OKINAWA KANASHII MONOGATARI

okinawa kanashii monogatari
the bird has been chained
to the sky
its tether stretching the pacific
crucified between the u.s. and jieitai
okinawa, okinawa
i who have loved you for so long
i weep for you
                    for you were the laughter
of my land
the island of smiles/ valleys of tears
okinawa
okinawa kanashii monogatari
until the rain sweeps away the tears
i am blind
until the voices of the dead
burns the asphalt jungles
                    okinawa kaiyo
until a hundred men become a thousand
                    ampo funsai/ ampo funsai
until the machines which convert
time into pain/ fields into graves
creak and rust into the past
                    there will be no songs
bird wings clipped, birds feet chained

TO MIRIKITANI

12-16-73

from bleakness
scratched out by
chicken claws you grew
too fast
tall dreams
reaching for more
than petaluma farms
breasts heaving to heavens
in search of unknown
until incestuous hands
ripped open
your white blouse

can you see my hand in love
reaching out to you/sister/
leaving you bare

still you grew
the only way out being
follow the rooster
tho ucla white boys are
all alike
always trying to out
voodoo the sun
your thin yellow body stood
out like jaundice
among the rooster's kind
"not normal . . . japanese . . . "
"not normal . . . " nakedly alone
leavin' us all slant eyed
nakedly bare as le trois monde

for your eyes of ebony
poems have borne
black red yellow brown
can you see my hand in love
reaching out to you/sister/
for our ancestral pain
born long before chicken farms,
roosters masturbate -
read between the lines
mirikitani means makibaka
for all your sadness
hold my hand and let me say
i understand.

CRAZY SOLILOQUY

part
2

the doorbell rings
i am madame butterfly
my hair is piled in a crown of black
above my eyes

my black top
cuts across my bosum with
the cross of a kimono
i am madame butterfly
i say to myself,
i say i reassure i talk
insanity a journey
into the confused
chambers of my soul
i must say, look -
look at your eyes in the mirror
are those not the same as madame butterfly?
does the stranger at the door see madame butterfly?
suzie wong?
either one -
does it make a difference to him?
look - look at yourself
can you see a woman who ran across three continents
seeking herself in the mirror
of someone else?
look at the spines of your eyelashes
do they drive you crazy
back in to the folds of your eyes
of your lips/nose/flower/
and the shadow in the mirror does not answer
the shadows of three continents do not answer
time remains at a standstill.

Alex Kuo

It took ten years of writing almost daily for me to discover that I must write slower, longer between poems, and longer poems. That meant I did not need to stay in practice, for most of whom I suspect it meant nothing more than the process being an end in itself anyway.

In the last five years I have concentrated more on things around me that interest me, particularly exploring the conventional group attitudes that are rooted in a history which most of us share, are trapped in, but is conveniently hidden from us, and hence distorting our understanding of ourselves.

Although this sort of discovery by going back to the source is in itself important, I have found that for me the process of discovery must also bring us at least to the present, to make some confrontation with the contemporary scene that will be freeing. Ultimately this is the only act that means anything, will make any difference.

I have also found that poetry has limitations for what I've been trying to do, and have consequently worked in short fiction forms, mostly pieces less than 1,000 words.

LOSS

It all began
with my fingers pressing
into the small
of your naked

back, or with yours
into mine when
(then) we both
moved moving against

each other's flesh
against the snow
under us, under
the snow melting

into the shape
of our bodies, as
did our hands
into, too

the shape of each
other's back. Or
was it the other
way around, with

the eccentric sense
of time
and place receding
beyond their abstract

in my present
knowing. I don't know
which for sure
now, or whether it

even ever
happened at all
then. Experience is
the hard loss

of language
and place beyond
time
(now) the impossible

location of a past
I can claim
no understanding
of, no, not

now, or then
or then returning
there, dying
there in the beginning.

PORTRAIT OF A NEGATIVE

1.
Limping to this spreading portrait
we came

the ill, some saints, the perverse, and
a few

with historical names, searching for
the flaw.

2.
With tears drowning in the night
overhead fan breaking black
glass, I search for originals
of negatives, black and white
plates of my grandparents, death
experts in their own right.

3.
The eye sees little that the mind
has not

known before: a hole in the wall
the blood

spreading down the bed, arrivals
departures.

4.
Their pools of blood settle
about my feet, closing
door shutting out sunlight
from abyss of bed slept
disinterestedly
inward after the murder
of love's lovemaking.

5.
Tell me this isn't so. Tell me
as I

stand near my own body, watching
old men

in their eccentric lie. Tell me
as I

watch this blood pulsing out of me.
Tell me.

6.
I can almost see
a bleached bird perched in
the distance where the
sun is limp and still
farther small bits of
yellowed photographs
showing the reverse
of what must have once
been true and oh yes
devoured and destroyed
even though perhaps
they came the closest.

7.
They are standing about me now
watching

trying to preserve some knowledge
for their

future, trying to retain an
image

of the past, of me, standing still
watching

me watching them, disregarding
that what

they now see as changeless was
never.

8.
light breaks in this prism
of the past guilt gnaws away
at flesh distant sound of
gunfire bodies fall apart
and I just want to lie
down in the blood and drowning
in my own body no
portrait to hold monument

GREEN TANKS AND OTHER HIDDEN VEHICLES OF DESTRUCTION

for Carroll Arnett

WASHINGTON–The demilitarized zone–the strip of land between the two Vietnams so crucial to diplomatic progress on the war–is in a comparative lull.

This reading by military officers came Thursday along with the official report from Saigon that Americans killed in the war totaled 177 for the week ending Aug. 17.

Military officers noting the lull in the DMZ were frank to say that nobody really knows where the enemy has gone from his old positions.

–UPI, August/68

Where the enemy has gone
nobody knows for sure. Yet
we wait for the miracle
a crucial lull weightless in
one dark end of the infinite.

(The beast, flaring napalm from
its bowels, crawls in the mud
the very jungle sucking
at its life. The energies
it burned have been turned into
stone forever, to be thawed
out of the cold stars at a
distant historic age. In
the meantime we twist sharpened
steel deep into the wounds of
the dead, and the half dead, to
the point of acceptance, in-
divisible arbiters
in the butchers' orphange.)

I too have sat in the house
of God and seen my enemy
disappear into the dark.

In the diplomatic lull
corpses are tagged and tallied
their torn mouths almost blackened
by the light we sometimes use
as mirrors for recognition.
Most faces bear no hatred
nor love; only the hidden
madness revealed on faces
in moviehouses when lights
had permitted us to see
ourselves. We move the bodies
touching their cold indifference.
There is no way to keep their
blood from sticking in my skin and
no single music to measure
the circumference of their wound;
only the shadows of my
footfalls being sucked deeper
and deeper down into those
dark positions of the past.

Alan Chong Lau

I came out of the only chinese restaurant in town somewhere in the mountains of northern california raised on fried rice and hamburgers and one grandmother from the province of canton. been to numerous schools, finally split the country and went around the world ending up in japan for a spell of four years. got into brushpainting. have now resettled outside of santa cruz adjusting to america and trying to learn how to paint all over again. all the poems come out of a work now in progress tentatively entitled *Songs for Jadina* , my grandmother, which hopefully will trace my family from origins in china to the pagoda restaurant in paradise calif. kazuko helps make things possible.

DREAM SONGS OF HAKA ANCESTORS

song one - origins

1.

by the river
they built huts

faces caked with mud
walking on hands and knees

pictures drawn in the earth
with fingers and toes
and the words were never wrong

they would nod by fire
cracking branches like music
tunes the mountain sent them

faces
the eyes of wanderers
ears hung flappy
as fat mushrooms

lips uncomfortable
in just one place
would begin moving
seeds spread to wind

one morning what left?
only pieces of fingers lips
soft chunks of lobes
threads of hair in water

huts mere crumbs of ash
sprinkled the sand with birthmarks

snakes of smoke slithered
thru tufts of grass

for the first time
one looked at sky
expecting rain

2.

the crows
return
dotting the shore
with slivers of noise

boys with slingshots
come down and kill
every single one

the water is bitter
clouds sour at the touch

barely scratching the mud
it runs in one thin trickle

bodies of crows
mingle there
where it stops
making a pile of feathery flowers

song two - haka woman *(for another haka woman, han suyin)*

no one would want you
for a concubine
you have big feet
that run down the road
not stopping for any man's privilege

not at home
with silk brocade
instead stand in the fields
beside the men
as they chase away crows
you run the waterwheel

big feet push
push and pedal
heaving a sigh
as the wheel revolves

tongue grows dry
as water laps out
licking moist each track of wood

long hair
untied down
plays catch with the wind

to match the rhythm
of big feet
pumping up   pumping down
you sing a song

"my lover going up to szechuan
boards the salt boat to chieh an
leaves my heart behind"

<u>SONG THREE</u> -- a search for taiping ghosts

1.

like a blind boy
on a train
not sure of destination
get off at every stop
to buy postcards
pasting them in a book of days

wind   sea   grass   fire   leaves
these form the other pages

if i were like others
i would be home now
instead blow
on a flute of bones
comforted by the sound

at night a path of light
crosses the river
taiping ghosts scurry over
melt into the gleam of blood red cliffs

i want to follow
but the boatman is afraid
to move the oar
"no one passes the tatu at night"

we sit in his hut
recalling the broken names
of our country's heroes

"have you heard of those
who defaced the altars
turned over the incense urns
drove coughing scholars out in smoke?"

he spits
piercing the head of a nail
above the washboard
nods as the moon nudges his head

"i have seen so many skeletons on the road
no longer can i sleep at night
have you seen those skeletons walking?"

2.

i love to hear the birds
sing the sun up
night's fingernails
carry the blood
of too many lice cracked in corners

daylight's fingers
are soft drumming mallets
of gold

lugging a watermelon to a village
i wear a hat of leaves
juicy thoughts plunder
my mind of any silence

last time i saw a woman
she had bells on her ankles
they sang as she ran
thru tall grass swishing

my thoughts on this
and i can't help but stumble
in the distance a water wheel
sings of it's own accord
tongues of water

the book i am writing
is full of postcards
addresses of vendors orphans barefoot peasants
people who don't exist

wind sea grass fire leaves
these form the other pages

SONG FOR MY MOTHER

the first song . . . . . . a faded snapshot

see this girl in the picture?
so fine
i would risk stabbing my chopsticks
in the rice
to get attention

outside
of a tenement
chubby feet planted
on separate wood planks
in buster brown shoes -
what are you doing?

a potted flower
in front
just watered
i imagine

on the left
more tenements
in a graceful swoon
similar in construction

one nail cannot
hold up dust for long

above
the next floor's balcony
juts out
a greco roman swirl lines the edge
nudging your head

the sun slices
thru the balcony
bouncing up a growth
of brown legs

those cheeks
fat enough to squeeze
smile about something being said

your white blouse
as yet unsmudged
is trembling

inside the heart of a tiny bird
sings the only song in chinese
you can remember

THE JANUARY OF 75

they had told me
greatgrand father
had come here
splashed his calligraphy
in the sanctum of an altar
the front window of a newspaper office
i never could get the story straight

he, along with countless others
not so famous as sun
had left china women children village
to gather support and anything else
they could get in the bargain

greatgrandfather
a cracked egg
an exile journalist
jotter of jumbled characters
where can your lines be?   heh?
                                        ah bok!
                                                    old man!

i ask the duckmarket
i ask ping yuen bakery (good pies)
i ask woy loey goey late night basement cafe (almond custard, good)
i ask mahjong parlour/ in backroom of the barbershop keno parlour
i ask year of the rabbit
i ask pig feet fisheye bittermelon beansprouts cha shu bow
i ask portmouth square

auperstitious of my english
they give no answers
not speaking chinese or pidgin
they look at me strangely
when i try reading the menu upside down

on the rim of chinatown
where all the oldtimers drop lugees
i find the street
expecting to find a newspaper office
an ancient scroll gathering dust
munching on dried up flies
in a display window
with perhaps a dead potted plant
to keep it company

the building is gone
a hamburger stand sits on the site
new calligraphy is everywhere
behind the counter
in the chinaman's pickmarked query
in the silver sprayed "lo fan eat shit"
on the parking rail
in the curls of greasetracks
on cheeseburger wrappers
on the windows of highrisers

i look at one point in the sky
the bank of america building
and dream of another kind of writing
when this city lies
completely leveled by nature's dance

this calligraphy of future lines cracks
accidental smiles
keeps me walking down the sidewalk
not turning back

Mbembe (Milton Smith)

I haven't been overly concerned with definitions as to what poetry is or how poetry is created. Initially I began writing because of an intense interest in black people and thought of my art as a message. Now as the black arts movement has encountered setbacks and much disintegration, I have become more concerned with my art as a serious way of life and expression of myself.

I want to draw out of myself and lay before the reader whatever is important about me and my thinking. I am concerned with floating free of ideology and similar restrictions by whoever would impose them. In spite of all the confusion in the sixties around a black esthetic and what it is/was, the problem for me is now resolved. Nobody has to write like me, I feel no obligation to write like others. I want to be accessible but not simplistic.

POEM

one
poem
that
i
wanted
to
write
about
black people was so beautiful
it would not even b a letter.

3 A.M.

like the stones
that beat the man down
are weathered
by the march
of rain to grimy lumps
then to dust.
there is no peace
we just come to a rest.

BLKNESS NO. 2

Blue quiet night
& the myth
of the lone highway
that bears nothing but travellers
like the splendor darkness
descent, descent in flight.
blue.
i was somewhere
in the night
on this highway
in the rain

& a quick lightning flash
& a star darkened
the way.

TREE

slim
city
winter
black
bark
angular
branches
it waits,
surrounded by concrete,
next to a bus stop
for elemental changes.
now!

THE WORLD IS A STUBBED TOE

Pick up my pen
I can write anything;
say the moon's
a round face yellow nymph,
that there's a heaven,
that I can slide down
a mile long razor blade
and not cut my ass,
that I can walk
thru a lion's cage
in a hamburger suit
and white bucks untouched,
                    fantasy shit.
but my pen stubs its toe
on this nigger reality
which is like cataracts
and old men.

BOY

In the doorway
a black child
he is a shadow
in night light.
his eyes
suck the ghetto in
as with a peppermint straw.
his loneliness is the replica
of my youth.

WHO'S WHO IN AMERICA

Dog is the brother
who went upside Jimmy's head
with a pool cue
about 8 dollars
that time in the pool hall.

OTHER BOOKS BY THE AUTHOR?

My poetry is poetry of the proletariat
by the proletariat and for the bourgeoisie.

Melvin B. Tolson

look, bored middle mania
this is all the bleeding
i can do. and even if i wrote
a novel, long spills that singed
your eyes, you'd say somebody else
said it better.

i don't find it childish
that scissors cut paper
or the least bit amusing
that i'm driven to write this stuff;
rage deterred
like a still life
of an apple
            and
                a hatchet.

SOMETHING ELSE THEY SAY

is that jazz is dead
but i want to tell you
that in a wooden loft in chicago
Archie Shepp gave artificial respiration
to a carcass.

no gimmicks,
no electricity coming from his sax,
just the naked instrument
that hung limp
from a thin red tie.

Shepp was dressed in a 1950 cotton suit,
faded and slick like rat fur.
when the sounds got good to him
he took off his coat
and turned to the band.
his hip pocket was snagged from years
of dragging a gin bottle.

as he blew
the words of critics flaked away.
the music they say is dead
was so alive, it sweated.

HIGH

friday night i stand with spread legs
on top of the house
& look down thru the night,
thru the roof beams
into the sleeping negro skulls.
& always lurking there
is the white boy's death.   come,
saturday night on the roof, i am
the blk god, Satchmo grown magnanimous
on hog maws, Muhammed Speaks
& some bush the panamanians
nurtured with gunpowder.
i shake my finger at the night,
pace the roof with my bible
clutched against my chest.
i hurl lightning at the suburbs.
then sunday morning i am there,
snow melting into house gutters,
my soul a mad man captured,
banging his head on the guilted air,
my body limp & peaceful.
the sound of billy graham
floats up from the radios
soothing me like a woman's hand.
& i am there on the roof
unable to brush my teeth
or take a shit,
wondering how i get down.

Jesús Papoleto Meléndez

Jesús Papoleto Meléndez was born in New York City. He attended the Fieldston School Upward Bound Program and Teachers and Writers Collaborative at J.H.S. 136. A school dropout, he returned to graduate from Morris H.S., studied at City College and Hunter College. His first book of poetry, *Street Poetry & Other Poems* was published by Barlenmir Press and his other books include *Have You Seen Liberation* and *Borracho.* His poems have been published by *The Rican Journal, Hanging Loose, Yardbird Reader, Screw Magazine,* and *The Greenfield Review.* He is also a playwright and his play, *The Junkies Stole The Clock* appeared off-broadway several years ago. He is now working on a novel entitled *The Autobiography Of The Planet Earth.*

& DOVES WERE NOWHERE TO BE FOUND

more bombs & planes/than birds & clouds
flew in skies   suns & moons had retired from,

doves were nowhere to be found,
& flowerchildren searched for broken wings.

& it was then that the world came to me   & said
in a voice i could easily understand   /in tears
it spoke/

help. help.

& i turned to the wind   who also spoke in tears
& through eyes which had long since given up looking
i looked again   /for one last long time
& again i saw   as i had seen before
:tears on the faces of broken dolls.
:reflections of bombs in the eyes of children.

& in a voice which had long since given up shouting
to ears & minds which had long since given up listening/
i softly answered/

help. help.

T.V. COMMERCIAL NO. 073

i saw a t.v. commercial, yesterday,
& it played back/backwards
in a nightmare. today
in the middle of the afternoon,

the white lady drove her husband to the airport
he opened the door,
kissed the kids good-bye.

the kids fought over who should be elected
to eat the ash tray
so she drove them to macdonalds'
to eat fried horsemeat, instead,
because that was her mentality.

but the announcer said/
when a woman has to be both, mother & father
in the same dream/she should make it easy.

i saw a t.v. commercial, yesterday,
& it played back/backwards
in a nightmare, today,
in the middle of the afternoon.

so i told mama
& she reminded me
that macdonalds' doesnt accept food stamps.

WILLIE BOBO WAS A BAAAA/AAD DUDE

willie bobo was a baaaa/aad dude.
:was the meanest/slickest/talk'nest
motherjumper
ever sang some harmony
under the cool shade of a street lamp.

:was the love'nest/tity-bumper
ever made crazy love
in the burning hot shadow of hallways/
leaning 'gainst mailboxes.

willie bobo was a legend in his time,

yeah!
willie bobo was a baaaa/aad dude.

sold himself some coke/ & smoke.
made a real big score.

got himself an el/d/ra/do
shot up the block/ 5 times
so you can check him out/ replay.
& that fine/ ass pussy. smiling
in the front seat. his fingers up her ass.
yeah!

his el/d was so big
he needed 2 blocks head/start
to make a turn.

yeah.
willie bobo was a baaa/aad dude.

& traveled.
had himself shit up his house/
the big one up the corner/
got from china/japan/mexico.
& clothes/ for days.
mamas would beg him for a lay.

:man/ he was living.

one time/
i asked him how he started/
looked down at me/ & said:
one time, one time,
i was a little kid/ like you.

& on cool summer afternoons/ played stickball
& lodies/
spun tops in the streets.

one time. one time.
i was a little kid
with big/ wide/ brown eyes.
& a smile. that was mine.

BEFORE THE BELL RINGS

how many lovers will be caught kissing/behind the auditorium
before the bell rings   in morris high school.

what juke box/No. 1/hit tune/oldie but goldie/song
do you play everyday in the fish n' chips
across the street,
bus stop.

how many dreams have you dreamed into   sharing cigarettes
with your toilet pass   /five minutes/
hanging out your back pocket.

how many stolen items are in your locker.
give them back   :they do not belong   to you.

joey/runs for president of the student body.
:soda machines
:longer lunch hours.

don't call me after six,
papi is home.

let me sign your autograph book
& i will tell you a story we will find new understandings for
tomorrow.

Tony Moreno

Born in Rincon, Puerto Rico 4/17/48. Raised in Hell's Kitchen and "El Barrio."

Basic education received from the University of the Streets.

Presently poet in residence of Manhattan Community College (self-proclaimed).

Published in *English Journal, Akwasasne Notes, Folio.* First book published in 1975 by Greenfield Review Press called *Of Stones and Tears.* P.E.N. award winner in 1975.

My poetry reflects commitment, communication, simplicity and a deep sense of origin, the first glimmer of light in what was thought to be a hopelessly dark tunnel.

SALSA

This is 46th street
salsa,

I see un
paso fino
horse
boogalooing down
9th avenue,

An old lady
with her yesterday
dreams
smiles and does
un mambo
to the beat of
my blood.

We communicate
through our
guaguanco
she gives me
her unfulfilled
dreams
and we go our
separate ways,
strangers, but
not really.

And the children,
son tan serios.

I see a little
three year-old
with curly
africano hair
and taino nose,
learning the
mysteries of flight
from a butterfly
with Mongo
Santamaria's directions
seeking refuge
in his ears.

A tiny girl
with a rainbow
in her head/
not knowing that
rainbows/ are not
allowed in this
sociedad/trying
to teach un
amerikan eagle
el merengue del coqui
instead of
the
national anthem.

everywhere/ritmo/rythem
ritmo y salsa . . .

WEALTH

You asked me
if i knew of
a way for you
to become rich

with something
that has never
been done
before.

Well,

if you could
teach a bullfrog
how to dance
un merengue

or compose
an orchestra
from crickets
with a
butterfly
conducting

or teach
a hawk
to sing
un guaguanco.

If you could
teach a broken
man
to smile

or if you
bottled rainbows
and gave them to
the somber
for a smile

If you could
teach
a leader
how to say
peace!
and mean it,

then i think
you would be
rich.

It's hard to do
something
that no one
has done
before. . .

MEMORIES

Yes, I still have
memories of
an island
in the sun

i remember a sad eyed
child
hanging on to the hem
of mi viejita's
dress
as she went to work
at la fonda
and drinking cafe
from coca cola
bottles

i had a dog named
tarzan
who climbed trees
after the lizards
but
he never caught one
they were too fast
or
he was too humane

i remember a shack
made from palm fronds
which the
centipedes and spiders
visited
at night

i remember a dream
i had
of finding cofresi's
treasure
and buying candy
with it,
and a toy
y the crowing of
the rooster,
or a house
for coqui

i remember pulling
el chinchorro y
stealing honey;
immortal
preoccupations of
a cipher. . . .

FOR YVONNE, MY DAUGHTER

When first
the sun smiled
for you

I looked
and saw
a tiny me

a jewel set
in my crown
of thorns,
a rainbow decorated
balsa cross.

Before the void
released
your soul
to play with
spring

we met.

I loved my cheek
pressed against
yours
a layer of
soon to be
dust
    between
            us. . . .

MIRACLE

If in your search
you come across a
deaf, dumb, blind
person

know that he is
truth,

And if you
come across a
mindless, crippled
one

know that he is
justice.

And if you
come across a
smiling, friendly
one
with eyes of
night
and breath of
yesterday

know that he is
death.

But if you
come across a
person
whose eyes shine
of tomorrow's
butterflys,

If he is colored
like the peacock
and smells like
all the flowers,

If he speaks
to you
in a strange/indian
tongue/of star
filled dreams
and things
that never were.

Follow his every
lead
he is the miracle
that you've been
searching for. . . .

FIRST READING

It was a night when all
the colors that constitute
un arcoiris
sat down and got
stoned on beer and words

Words, sometimes funny
sometimes happy,
a veces triste.

Americo's sad tones saying
good-bye to a brother
with Falcon's bajo
dripping tears

Papoleto's angry voice
chipping away at the
foundations of wilfredo
Y Joe's words painting
indios.

On this night Tony flapped
his wings
disturbing the dust
of his forefathers,
and they smiled

Tomorrow there will be
one less silent shadow
porque
tony got his wings.

Nashira N'tosha

Nashira N'tosha is a young poet whose work, prior to its acceptance for this anthology, had never appeared in print. Jessica Tarahata Hagedorn has described Ntashira Ntosha's poetry as being "highly original, rhythmic and moving." Not only a writer, but a filmmaker, Ntashira Ntosha was born in New York City twenty-eight years ago. She has been living in the Bay area for about seven years now, and has been actively involved in Third World media. She is now working for the radio station KPFA-FM in Berkeley.

PHANTOMS

who are these phantoms of men
who used to be
warriors, princes, dancers

squat in squalor's trousers
bathing in the feces
of concrete dogs
dining in automats
on unemployment rolls

who are these spectres of queens
who danced in veils
used to be
mistresses, daughters, blue skeins
slithering in streets
lounging in the mud
of cosmetic wonders
waiting for the key to make the turn

women drove the horse carts
loaded wagons with dirt
hoisted their skirts
and mixed rich earth hues
with our mother

don't forget our backs
our tortoise hulls
our bows and arrows
back and spine
that which keeps us
deliberate

makes us fast and clever

who are we
dreaming up new colors
to paint planets
bessies,
billies,
miles?

blue-blacking our intonations
housekeeping the silver secrets
choosing between
construction work
and god

men burn our houses down
in alabama and guinea-bissau,
steal our dogs,
put death
in our woman wombs

who this is
got us washing with soaps
made from the sperm
of just old men

who this is
kills our fathers,
drives us to their schools
as if they were hospitals

drives us to their schools
as if they were hospitals

bessie have wings -
woman wings

what is this
used-to-be . . .
long-walkin' down voodoo highways

orishas
saints
goddesses

handclappin' for the obeah
etherin' for the inner soul
vapor dust
magnetizin'
for the millions

THIS SITE IS OCCUPIED

(for the art ensemble of chicago)

this site is occupied
by everyone in sight
if there was room to dream
walls would have wings
and split

time enough
to give a look
every second

the every first time
in spite of tricks
that fools engender
swimming too close
to the bottom

true underwater bliss
is in the bell of lester bowie
silver fans
move my fingers
across the sea.

this site is occupied
by everyone in sight
my fingers touch the wind
and conjure him

funk me down now
toward silver fishes
the long lake
with every ripple
tempobleeding
into another free look
at ourselves

wings are flashing
shaker cymbal of quaco the slave
boogaloo boogaboo
every witch away
listening to the wizard touch

malachi
the way your head moves
in tune to mali

makes me smile

IT'S FUNNNY YOU SHOULD MENTION THAT

it's funny you should mention that

    hello baby   it's okay   you real
        i mean, ain't you? you there and i'm smiling

him. . . he's just a rumor. . .

i mean it ain't like he can play basketball like kareem

and blow more trumpet than i got brains
him. . . he's just a rumor. . .

        sugar   a funky one at that   yeah

i mean, low -- his odor make slaughterhouses seem sweet

                low, i mean
and can't hold his own when it comes to something ain't his
so that's why i say
    it's kinda funny you should mention that
now really
        how many folks doin' anything
                                    can make conversation
                                            with the dead

soothe the hungry   put africa back   on the map
cause amen-ra to make a play for a re-run
counsel the wicked to poison themselves without knowing

sigh and inflate the planet
but anyway   just the same   it's funny you should ask

cause it ain't none of yr goddam bizness   what i was doing
since you been gone,
sweet sweet darlin'

Simon Ortiz

I was talking with a young Acoma man, a Vietnam vet, this afternoon. We've been working at Acu around the village and at the mission. He was chuckling, saying, "Those old men, they talk about everything. They were talking about the wheat deal with Russia and now they're talking about Marilyn Monroe." The older Acoma men were standing by the mixing trough. Some younger men were mixing mud and carrying it to the men building and plastering a wall.

That's the thing about human expression, the variety and spectrum of things they talk about, the all-inclusive perspective that they have. Earlier, they had been talking about the value of work -- while standing idly around -- and long haired hippies and the Beatles and music they couldn't understand. And then they talked about the rain falling at the moment. "It is beautiful," one of them said, and another added, "If only it could be like this all the time." They looked around them and pointed to the west, and one of them said, "It has already come out," meaning the floodwater from the mountainous upslope west of Acu where it was raining earlier. "Hah uh, you can tell because it's shining," another said. Some of them have fields of corn and pumpkins over that way, and they were happy about the rainfall.

This is the thing about the language that I write out of, I think, the all-inclusiveness. I have listened to these men for ages it seems -- well, for years. They talk about everything, a lot of gossip -- some vindictive, some mainly humorous -- a lot of sex -- there has to be always that -- and a lot about "new" things and ways they don't always understand nor would ever really want to know fully about. They reminisce, and they speculate a lot, but there is always that finely tuned perspective that they have. They see, I think, the core of the way things are, that undercurrent of truth running through human events and meanings

These are the men who keep up the traditions of our people, community, of our language. These are the people who insure that the language keeps being a way of *touching* among ourselves, the things we see and hear, the things that we all are enjoined with, those things around *all* of us.

They knew language as a true way of knowing themselves. They talk, and I listen and I listen, and I listen. And later, I try to write it down with that perspective.

INDIAN GUYS AT THE BAR

My head is drawing closer to the bar again
when someone says,

"Damn, my wife just lost her job,
I don't know what to do."

"Sometimes I drink;
other times I think I'm just crazy."

"Hey, here comes Jim. God, he's ugly."

"That's okay, brother, sit down.
Chippewas are always like that."

"Yeah, Chippewas were made to be like that."

The words jerk through me;
they vibrate and wobble for a long time.

"If them Pueblos ever learn to work,
they'll be okay."

"It's a cultural trait with them,
climb cliffs and throw rocks,
too tired to work."

"I heard three Indian guys got stabbed
downtown outside the Winstins.
Someone was watching them from the Federal Building
from the sixth floor where the BIA is."

Silence is sometimes the still wind;
sometimes it is the emptiness.

"I went to see my parole officer;
he said to behave or we'll send you back to the res."

"Man, when I was about to get out,
I heard the guard yell, '0367 Griego,
get your red ass in gear, you're going home,'
I couldn't believe it; I just stood there and cried."

"I know. I know. Here, have another drink
of culture."

I don't know if my feet can make it;
my soul is where it has always been;
my heart is staggering somewhere in between.

THE EXPECTANT FATHER

I am an expectant father.

Pray then:
  smile for all good things
  note the wind
  note the rain
  touch the gentleness with care
  be good

After we had watched the hawk circling in the hot wind and lost it against the color of the mesa across the valley, we decided to climb down the mesa to this spring. We walked for about half a mile and finally arrived there. The spring is in a cave made by two huge slabs of sandstone cliff leaning into each other. The water dripped from soft crumbly sandstone and ran into a small pool before it. Around the water were handhigh green ferny plants and moss grew on damp stone. There were movements in the water which were our reflections and tiny waterbeings that live there. Earl dipped into the water with a rusty can and drank and then Gilly. It was my turn then. The spring water tasted sweet and of underground stone, but something of a taste that was more like a touching wind than anything else. There was something else too, something else. We were quite young then. We weren't so tired and hot after a while anymore, and we climbed on down to that flat valley and looked some more for our horses.

When the child comes, expectant father,
tell the child.

When I have awoken in the early morning, I have felt the child's flutter at the small of my back. The child's mother pressed against me. The child is a butterfly cupped in the earth mother's hand. Feel. Be gentle, *naya*, be kind, this morning and for all mornings of your child's life.

When it rains in a soft wind,
it feels so good.

SOME 5-DAY DRUNK POEMS

The Poet

"Are you really a poet?"

"Shore."

Crickets always talk like that.

A couple nights after,
I listened for a long time
to a couple reminding themselves
about 10 million years ago
in some cave in Asia;
it was a long, long time ago;
they rattled membranes together
and sang all night long.

"I didn't know you were a poet."

Later on,
there was another cave.
A woman was moaning,
and later she was laughing,
not very far from a glacier's edge.

To the south were swaying grasses,
brightly colored birds, warm oceans,
hot deserts, and strange gods
who demanded nothing.

She asked me if I liked crickets.
I said, Yeah, but not cockroaches.
I wonder out loud
if cockroaches are any relation
to crickets, maybe, but not close.
Want to look it up somewhere.
10 million years is a hell of a long time
to really clear it up.

"How long you been a poet?"

It is late at night, lying drunk on the floor, hearing
a church bell across the street, remembering that Wisconsin
horse this Spring:

One step at a time to return.

The horse across the road
stands within a fence,
silent in the hot afternoon.

A mile north is some construction.
I tell the horse,
That's America building something.

A mile further through a clump of trees
is a river.

The Wisconsin horse is silent.

The Bell clamors
against the insides of my skull.
It has nothing to do with sound
that can comfort.

The clamor wants to escape
its barriers;
I want it to escape;
I have no defenses.

I should be an eager Christian
hungry for salvation;
or at the very least accept snugness
bound tightly in clear plastic.

Yet, at this single point in my life,
I know only a few bare things:
the floor, the walls around me,
and that bell across the street,
that despair is a miserable excuse
for emptiness,
that I should echo louder
that call for salvation
which at this point I know
is a need to fill the hollows
and pockets of my body.

But now and soon,
in this dark night,
having gotten up to write
this offering:
that Wisconsin horse I saw
standing in the hot afternoon
staring through a chainlink fence
at the construction going on
only a mile away,
I wonder now
if the horse still stands silent in the dark night,
dreamless and stifled, having no recourses left
except to hope his silence will soon go away
and the meaningfulness enter.

JULY 12

Today is the third day.
It will rain.
Soon.
Pray then, be calm, don't worry.

Notes for the Child: written July 5, 1973

Woke slow this morning.

Hear Joy moan,
stir around,
and get up sometime after 5.

Bit of morning light.

Get up and wash,
put on 2 day-old coffee.

Later,
we walk for you
over to University Drug.

Sun slants
through trees,
cool a.m.

See two cicadas:
one is dead; the other is buzzing,
trying to take off
from the sidewalk.

I want to turn back
and help it -
fly again -
but I realize
the inevitable.

Yesterday while chopping weeds,
I uncovered two thumbsized burrows,
the cicadas not yet flown,
curled up, medium soft,
in their shells, yet.

Get to the hospital,
the taxi driver says, Goodluck.
Okay.

Hospitals are consistent,
crummy.

We wait for someone
to notice us

I tell Joy
to make herself visible.
She can't be any more visible,
she thinks than now,
her belly sticking out.

I ask where my wheelchair is
when Joy gets in hers,
pushed down the hall
and into an elevator
by a fat unsmiling aide.

Upstairs into a hall
and Joy disappears
behind some doors.

I squat on the tile floor,
and remember a poem Joy has written
about the story teller.

The aide walks by
and she smiles this time,
says, Okay.

I say, Okay, too.

Seven other people wait,
make small talk.
A couple women
are rolled by.

I smile at the six women
and one guy,
a couple smile back.

When the women are rolled by,
everything becomes somber
and slow.

. . . . the Wisconsin horse
is silent, looks through
the chainlink fence,
the construction going on
a mile away. . . .

Finally get to join Joy;
she's getting anxious,
can tell in her eyes,
movements, tremble
about her mouth.

A nurse tells me
to go to Admitting.
A girl asks me a question,
Are you the responsible party?
I say, Yes.
She means money, of course,
who's gonna pay?
I mean I'm the father
of the child bringing luck
and continuance.

Go back upstairs.
A woman on the other side
of the room moans a bit,
struggles in her sheets;
an older woman
holds her hand.

Joy is pretty relaxed,
breathes to make it easier –
amazing how anyone can relax
at the eve of birth --
only a stop along the way,
of course --
I ask Joy
if it hurts,
realize it's a dumb
but important question.

A doctor comes along
and puts a plastic machine
against Joy's belly
and flicks it on.

The doctor calls it
a doptone and says,
Don't ask me why it's called that,
I don't know. It runs on batteries.

I call it:
steady, gentle beating noises,
called flesh, bones, blood,
runs on spirits and mysteries
and dreams.

I'm hungry now,
but atmosphere of the hospital
prevents any real hunger,
the repressiveness of institutional
insulation, I figure.

Tell myself to relax, say,
When you come out, child,
let's go dance in a while, okay.

Look out the window
and see the sun
and the parking lot.

Wish I had a cigarette,
wish I had a beer,
wish I had some really new words.

Remembered that I wanted to write
something about that old dog,
kinda skinny and pathetic,
been hanging around our home
for a while, a week or so,
write some story about it.

. . . . and then she was born.
I will tell her about the Wisconsin horse.
She was born then. . . .

"She's as pretty as a silver dollar,"
said Ed Marlow, a miner in Eastern Kentucky
about Caroline Kennedy.
"She's just plain folks."

Abermarle Co. Sheriff says,
"We found nekkid women
with nekkid pubic hair
offensive."

July 5, 1973 is now and soon enough.

To Insure Survival:

You come forth
the color of a stone cliff
at dawn,
changing colors,
blue to red,
to all the colors of the earth.

Grandmother Spider speaks
laughter and growing
and weaving things and threading them
together to make life to wear,
all these, all these.

You come out, child,
naked as that cliff at sunrise,
shorn of anything
except spots of your mother's blood.
You kept blinking your eyes
and trying to catch your breath.

In five more days,
they will come,
singing, dancing,
bringing gifts,
the stones with voices,
the plants with bells.
They will come.

Child, they will come.

Wendy Rose

I'm Hopi and currently am attending UC Berkeley (about to graduate and am applying to graduate school); am majoring in both anthro. & Native Amer Studies which provides some of the electricity for my poem appliances. I feel that maybe someday soon I'll begin to write poetry, as for now I'm still growing up. I am 27 years old; will be 28 by the time this is in print. Going on 50 feels like. am dividing my time between studies, managing museum bookstore in berkeley, and coughing -- and also write and paint. Everything in print is out of date as of the day it comes out. I think the univ is driving me crazy (that's university not universe). But I guess it's okay because I've survived another year. Am publishing in field of anthro as well as poetry now, but that probably doesn't interest anyone. Am caught between skins that think I'm too white, whites, that think I'm too Indian (tried to pass for white as teenager; didn't work); also caught between being Indian working in museum and not trusted by white anthros, but at the same time not trusted by Indians because associated with anthros. Neither one has any idea how little the other trusts me but all I really want to do is live this life doing the best I can like everybody else.

Poems reflect all of above I guess but I think the urban/reservation, red/white in one body, anthro/NAS conflicts override all else at this time. Am looking for acceptance somewhere; not successful. Wonder if I'll survive another year. I live in berkeley but spend more time in el cerrito and richmond. have been doing lots of readings lately, but always in "3rd World" context. I don't feel like a "real" person because all of these labels are only confusing me. I just write.

LOVING

the pottery goodness
of my body
    settled down on flowers,
    pulling pollen in great
    handfuls; full & ready
    parts of me are pinned
    to earth, parts of me
    undermine song, parts of
    me spread over water, parts
    of me form a rainbow arch,
    parts of me follow the
    sandfish, parts of me are
    a woman who judges.

HUPA TWINED PENDANT: A WHITE WOMAN SPEAKS

Owl Woman's years and twisted hands lie
arthritic between my breasts, twined into shapes

momentary as sound, forever as willow-heart; shell and pine-nut
hoop, frog-egg strips breathing air too soon, and

as to who made it, who knows? not the Owl Woman Mother of N
and keeper of the way as I have said, but "nobody

just the indians" you say.

NATIVE AMERICAN STUDIES, UNIVERSITY OF CALIFORNIA AT BERKELEY 1975

Grandmother holds my hand so as
to be born again as bride-shawl reeds in
mid-dance;   she touches my legs,
becomes wind, blows devils to the mesa.

Like me she is scarred, like me
riding high on her fear, like me licking
labored north-eyes shut and feeding on
rock and water.

She is with me now, trembling in my throat, wearing poems,
confused with the pride of our dance, our dance itself proud
swinging through the seasons
between the eyes of two worlds that
never match, can only stare stupid and grey.

This cluster of tongues, this dark flying world,
this trying-on of the whiteman's witchery
stretches the Grandmother's skin.

Shuffling Butterfly she
takes me
away.

FOR RON TANAKA AT STANFORD

(a return to pinpoints)

He labors

his love a birth-labor, his
songs long rope that
pulls stars about to where they
can weep unmolested
by culture

Tanaka Tanaka
like the best Hopi silver
your soul is a secret
inlaid so deep it takes
knowing caves to
see it. Some of us come in

and sight along the edge to
fall softly absorbed in your
bones   in our sleep we
are layered
into Sensei love

how you sing those
old mountain songs

VANISHING POINT: URBAN INDIAN

It is I in the cities, in the bars, in the
dustless reaches of cold eyes who vanishes, who leans

underbalanced into nothing; it is I without learning
I without song, who dies & cries the death time, who

blows from place to place hanging onto dandelion dust,
dying over & over. It is I who had to search & turn the stones,

half-dead crawl through the bones, let tears dissolve the dry caves
where woman-ghosts roll piki & insects move to keep this world ali

It is I who hold the generous bowl that flows over with shell & stc
that is buried in blood, that places its shape within rock carvings.

It is I who die bearing cracked turquoise and making noise
so as to protect your fragile immortality O Medicine Ones.

THE RED/WHITE BLUES (bicentennial special)

Never so strong as to fly unassisted, I have left
so much pain on this world that it heaves over
no longer elongating its crystals, blooming its trees,
lambing its ewes.

What passed once as leaf twisted onto plaster
is bloodless -- I know of "passing",
I know of bloodlessness.

The solid creekwater shapes a chrysalis for its children
into which they will back without human doubts,
without wondering if flesh is real or
if what lies under can die.

I would burrow with them: had I my father's badger-claw,
my mother's buckeye-basket
but the poisons throughout my soul are
not to be leached with water.

I lose count of those elements
that pad me with mud.

Ricardo Sanchez

Ricardo Sanchez, born in El Chuco (nee El Paso), Tejaslum, raised in El Barrio del Diablo (the Devil's Ward in the Eastside), and schooled in such undergraduate enclaves as Chino & Soledad (California Prison System) & the Huntsville & Ramsey I Prison Farm (Texas Department of Deformation)--high school push out and pinto/poet/writer/bato loco bien chuco,

also Ph.D. graduate from Union Graduate School (Yellow Springs, Ohio), author of *Canto y Grito Mi Liberación/The Liberation of a Chicano Mind* (Doubleday Anchor Books), *Obras* (Quetzal-Vihio Press), *Mano a Mano* (Bruto Publications), *With Una Raíz toward the Sun* (Mixtec-Verga Publishing Co.), *Los Cuatro* (Barrio Press), and *Hechizospells* (Aztlan Publications, UCLA).

ay, from the penury of the barrio to the anomie of prison to the madness of poetry written in the fusion of languages and cultures to also being a Ford Graduate Fellow twice, a Frederick Douglass Fellow in Journalism, ever an activist in the Chicano Movement, to the jiveyness of teaching poetics and lecturing and reading from Yale to Stanford to the Navajo Community College at the Navajo Nation at Tsaile...to being born no. 13 in a family tracing its roots back to the 1500's in Northern New Mexico (Indio-Hispano-Chicano/Mestizo, maternal grandmother born in San Juan Pueblo), to also being named Poet/Writer in Residence (till May, 1976) at the El Paso Community College by the National Endowment of the Arts...

ay, also editor for *La Puz Magazine* (Denver), *De Colores* (Albuquerque), *Chicano Light & Power, Inc.,* (Clap/El Paso), Míctla Publications (El Chuco), *Nalgahuatl Notes & Cábula* (an academic quarterly), to free lance writer/consultant/writer/lecturer to being alive and able to love freely both life and women and family...ay, let there be a *cantogrito* breaking any chains that might enslave anyone--for both women & men must have the freedom to create their own lifestyles and ways of being alive, vibrant, and liberated...

DRUM

drum of my people,
chicano drum
beating out sounds
from barrio and campo,
universal sound
                tun-tun-pa,
                ca-tum-ba, ca-tum-ba,
drum beat
signalling
beginning of life
when america was green
and life abounded hopefully
before machine fire
ate up
grasses and clear water,
before the coming of white waves
devouring all before them;
chapulin lived
near coyote
when nahuatl words
flowed
into mescalero/tewa idioms
and mestizo was a word
yet to be invented. . .
he came into our lives
merging his beard with our faces,
and his names were
spanish steel and toledo credulity,

still, he came unto the land,
called it tierra
and it uplifted his tiredness,
he lived
without fences
and fiercely proclaimed his rights;

later, much later, after
mestizo became
a people
who merged under the sun,

others came
wantonly to despoil,
                        not just conquer,
all that stood before them. . .

coyote then was lynched,
wantonly assassinated,
even foolishly hated,
and the tierra spewed up
rotted senses
of all that had been life;

drum of my people
predating
all that now exists,
silenced
like the cry
of empty city streets;
drum
that used to sound
like the thunder of the rain,
now impotently lying there
amidst the memories of mankind,
un-used
like thoughts and hopes
in a tierra just abused --

        somos nada mas
        que un pensamiento
        awaiting the fulfillment
        of that codex called chichitl
when the people of the sun
arise anew to be
a human providence
reclaiming back the earth. . .
and you will sound again
a majestic human call
to all that we must be. . .
                ca-tum-ba, ca-tum-ba,
                tun-tun-pa,
                ca-tum-ba, ca-tum-ba,
                tun-tun-pa. . . . .

TOWARD

toward, toward, ever toward,
that infernal struggle to present
all the awesome realities of being;

lost, being, yet lost,
within the wintry madness
of marginal existence, looking
inwardly to find
that sentient sense
of my having been
more than an after-thought. . .

soy como rayo de luna
radiantemente enluzando
las cavernas
donde mi raza duerme

unaware that there can be more,
for it hurts to seek
and need
a jelling place
in which to express

que tengo que vivir
fuertemente/totalmente,
como un pedazo de la historia. . .

I dreamt you last night
when far from your being i slept:
your lips caressed the sadness
gestated by separation,
o raza ardiente Chicana
you continue hauntingly existing
even here in this frozen nadir,
and a plethora of lies
lie furtively to my mind;

no se puede decir
que solo existo
cuando nos vemos;

no se puede admitir
que solo vivo
cuando nuestras realidades
curten los momentos
y cuando nos vemos cercas
en los espejos de nuestras mentes. . .

yes, look at my many faces,
all the colors of my people
radiate out,
some scorched by the sun
and others
turbulently scowling,
yet i am
the silken facets of being. . .

and when we seek out
a reason for being,
looking back atavistically
at a past merging

all the realities
that we have been,
seeing our boredom becoming
the blood of pyramid and adobe hut,
and my language becomes another world,
and we converge
here from all the nation
to intone
all that we can be,
es mas
que momentos
compartidos sobre cerverza y plática,

it is realization
seeping into mind and soul,
affirming that we can co-exist
but only if we care . . .

so the struggle comes on,
furious struggle demanding
total capitulation,
the loss of all i've been,
relegating roots and causes
to a dust-bin in the mind . . .

manic questions assail,
you, juan chicano or jaime boricua,
or robert chinee or richard injun,
any blackman or any other
name that projects out
your marginality,
just what in hell
can you presume to be?
can you be a universal latin
singing out
the history of the oppressed?
or piano playing oracle
hosting
poet madness
amidst jack daniels drinking
with words of ease?

or generalizing teacher
striving to up-root/deracinate
minds and souls
from their sense of land,
and subtly announce
that only your way is right?

mod hollywood producing chicano
merged into asian fantasy
mixt
(irrevocably)

with mandates
from a concert master,
stomped out into symphony
that cacophonously proclaims
that somehow we must merge
and lose the differences
that make us
a diverse and human world. . .

lost, my perdidos
andamos versiculando
bellezas
dormidas
como nuestras mentes . . .
and when we rap of barrio lives --
discarded
shards of non-technological perceptions --
we seek out those anchors
stabilizing
our anomic wandering selves,
and like all shipwrecked losers
we strive to standardize
feelings that know no measures,
for we exist as we exist,
but some get paid to standardize
and some do it out of fear
that without foundations laid by others
life will lose its meaning . . .
fear of dispossession
guides and ridicules our being,
living as i live,
knowing something is wrong
when i can dare to think
if only to myself
"thank god i don't exist
saying
god help me i'm ethnic,"

but truth it is,
for like all the people that i am,
i feel the need to be
much more than i can be,
lost and hurting that i am,
i view my loneliness
like others see their lives
                i am a shadow of my thoughts. . . .

Ntozake Shange

Ntozake Shange lives in San Francisco & New York alternately. She was educated at Barnard College & USC, receiving degrees in American Studies. She dances with Raymond Sawyer's Afro-American Dance Experience and has produced a choreopoem *For Colored Girls Who Have Considered Suicide,* the title of her collection of poems from Shameless Hussy Press this winter. Ms. Shange's work has appeared in *Third World Women, Time To Greez, Black Scholar, Margins, Mosaic, Anon., & The Plumb Press.* Her novel, *Sassafrass, Cypress, & Indigo,* is being published jointly by Shameless Hussy Press & Heirs Press in SF.

CROSS OCEANS INTO MY HEART

all i know is his name/ is james or jim/ shortened
somebody very very black & tall
so-phisticated for that time/ fore the war & he waznt
born here/ either/ born in paris/ carried to detroit when he
waz five/ a french-speakin niggah in detroit/ say 1926/

& he waz intense

a rich colored boy in the Depression
a pouter/ a brooder/ who took a wife
who didnt like just men in ohhhh/ maybe 1943

he hadda boat floatin in the detroit river
served in korea/ gotta be a physician/ did abortions
for girls bout my age when i waz in high school/

i know he owned bars by wharfs & up from transient
hotels/ he dealt smack/ & never hadda son
i always wanted to meet him

when he waz in college he usedta pay his friends
  to look after him while he waz out/
    he waz suicidal

    (my daddy & his girl rode in the backseat
    of the newest & hottest car in nashville
    on the way to where fletcher henderson might
    be/ some all colored spot/ & he/ jim wd
    buy lotsa whiskey/ & listen/ & seem to be
    treatin daddy & his girl/ who waz poor/
    but they were workin/ really/ makin sure/
    jim didnt kill everyone/ thinkin he waz
    mad music/ another kinda dangerous miles
    davis/ an impersonal assassin of his own love/
    so daddy & his girl rode in the front seat/
    on the way back from anywhere/ & jim lay
    molten in his back seat)

& he wd stay in his room until his parents left campus or
  till his wife's lover left town

(everybody knew abt her/ that she liked
to touch women's legs/ & mouths/ that
there waz nothin cd be done/ cuz she
had connections/ & he waz so sharp &
he took her/ & the sorority took her/ &
there was nothin cd be done/ cuz she waz
beautiful/ & then there he waz/ & wd
you mess wid him who is anger/ a
malignant fury/ in his glance/ when
someone wanted to say/ what everybody
knew abt her/ & did leave them alone/
& how cd he not know/ & if he did know
it must be he is really a foreigner/ not
a whole man himself/ to have a woman so/
a woman/ so fulla beauty/ she shared when
a breeze fell from her hands/ he never
left her)

i waited & waited to meet him

jim waz almost my daddy's best man/ but he cdnt come
cuz sometin came up/ daddy said waz a connection/ an
important deal/ not to be investigated further. . .

mama said she waz scared of him cuz
they all three/ drove 1500 miles or more
from nashville to ann arbor & jim didnt
say but two words/ 'yes' & 'idont know'
& he laughed/ like a jackal/ she said
cuz daddy actually took her to a ywca
& i have just found out how i waz in love
how i waz in love wid this man who has died
& i never knew him to touch
i never saw a picture/ but not far from me
not far from me/
never far from me/ i've kept a lover
who waznt all-american who didnt believe & wdnt straighten
up to standard & i've loved him like auntie emma victoria
loved joe louis/ who kicked that kraut into the mat/ & how
grandma viola loved nat king cole for havin the first
15 minute television show for colored/ first in the world/

& oh how i loved him for not ever believin in america/
he wd have none of it/ none of fisk/ none of cadillacs/
none of alphas & omegas/ none of virginal miz good family/
& none of hope/ none of their hope/ to make/
america real/ly sing a colored song/

oh watch my face getta mad tinglin kisses
is the same spirits usedta kiss him/ when he waz
marchin himself inta our pain/ lingerin in screams/
persistent/ hammers/ feet/ railroads/ needles/ horses/
women/ goldwatches/ & scotch/ flushin toilets/ twisted
fingers/ & somebody wantin to disregard him/
wantin to snub him/ wantin to act better/ cleaner/
in this filth/ gonna wipe shit evenly cross their faces/
steada careless/ & get uppity/ he isnt fit/ he isnt/
one of us/ & the horns he loved to hold him/
blew-pushed-away-stupidness/

i've loved him
in my own way/ in my own men/ sometimes hateful/
sometimes subtle like fog in high skies & sun/ but
you know who you are/ who i cherished in you isnt real
is not believin/ i loved yr bitterness & hankered after
space in you where jim's fury swept round like
cab calloway's band in '3*D'/ where you are outta control/
where you cannot touch/ or you wd kill me/ & somebody else
who loved you/ that's what i wanted/ yr roots throttlin
possibly song/ & no hope/ i desperately loved sharin yr
refusal to believe in this place/ & ohhh what poems
we have/ what none babies & separate houses/
leanin on lil sticks of anger/ it waz him i sought out/
wd search forever thru any arms/ any sound/ of not willin to die
mistaken for an american

& i'm sorry/ i'm sorry/ i cdnt see
those mountains dense & heavin/ dry heaves in my stubby hands/
refused to take my murders on myself/
i've got em now/ all of it/ all the love i slew off me/
all the whiskey/ all the lies/ & the poems/
they run up & down my skin like rabid hyenas/ & you
didnt know him either/ we were too smart to meet him/
too aware of our craziness/ wd get outta hand/ if
we let him in/

(when we were marchin the streets gainst
the war/ he waz gettin arms to guinea-bissau/
when we were layin up in school halls kissin/
he waz takin fetuses outta nine year old
girls/ who didnt know/ how much they were
gonna hurt/ & he waz smitten/ smitten early)

so he died on a boat/
in the water/ no heirs/ & i love him
celebrate wid him/ bein free of this/ bein not here/
layin in salt & bones of others who refused to unfurl the flag
those others who knew bein colored in america waz time-released suicide

(before he died/ jim tried to sell my daddy
the boat/ go on p.t./ he said/ it's worth
it/ take it man/ & my daddy/ bein an
american didnt understand/ but i knew
what he meant/ & i've taken him unto me/
i hold him at night/ & become all the
music he cd have known/ i hold him/
& whisper other tongues/ i sing simple
songs of hope/ & i cry & tear up my
clothes/ or the poems inta the street/
& i drink til i'm sick/ or sit up for
days & nights/ in mournin/ with a dry
mouth/ & no tears)

i never even saw a picture
& i've loved him all my life
he is all my insanity
anyone who loves me will understand

GRADUATION NITE

(for carol lee/ que linda mujer)

graduation nite &
i waz the only virgin in the crowd
bobby mills martin jerome & sammy yates
eddie jones & randi
all cousins
all the prettiest niggahs in this factory town
carried me out wid em

in a deep blk buick smellin of thunder bird &
ladies in heat
we rambled from camden to mount holly
laughin at the afternoon's speeches & danglin our tassels
from the rear-view mirror/
climbin different kinda project stairs
movin toward snappin beer cans &
GET IT MAMA THAT THE WAY TO DO IT

all mercer county graduated the same nite
cosmetology secretarial pre-college auto-shop & business
all us movin from mama to what ever
waz out there
that nite
we raced a big ol truck from the barbeque stand
tryin to tell him bout the party at jacqui's
where folks graduated last year waz waztin
to Hit It wid us
i got drunk & cdnt figure out whose hand waz
on my leg but it didnt matter cuz these cousins
martin randy eddie sammy jerome & bobby waz my sweethearts
alternately since the 7th grade
& everybody knew i always started cryin if
SOMEBODY TRIED TO TAKE ADVANTAGE OF ME

at jacqui's
ulinda mason waz stickin her mouth all out
while we tumbled out the buick
eddie jones waz her lickin stick/
but i knew how to dance
it got so hot/
vincent ramos puked all in the punch & harley jumped all up
in tico's face cuz he waz leavin for the navy in the
mornin/ had to kick ass/ so we'd all remember
how bad he waz/

seems like sheila & marguerite waz fraid to get their hair
turnin back so they laid up gainst the wall
lookin almost sexy
didnt wanna sweat
but me & my fellas we waz dancin/

since 1963 i'd won all kinda contests
wid the cousins at POLICE ATHLETIC LEAGUE DANCES
every other saturday night/
all mercer county knew any kin to martin yates cd
turn somersaults before smokey robinson cd get a woman excited/
&
we danced doin nasty oltricks i'd been thinkin
since may cuz graduation nite had to be hot &
i waz the only virgin
so i hadta make like

my hips waz inta some business
that way everybody thot whoever waz
gettin it waz a Older Man cdnt run the streets w/ youngsters

martin slipped his leg round my thigh
martha & the vandellas bumped HEAT WAVE
up & down up & down the new carver homes

WE WAZ GROWN

WE WAZ FINALLY GROWN

ulinda all of a sudden went crazy
went over to eddie cursin & carryin on
tearin his skin wid her nails/ the cousins tried to hold
her arms/ tried to talk sense to her/ listen bitch/ sammy went on

bobby whispered i shd go wid him fore they gotta cuttin/
fore the police arrived
we teetered silently thru the parkin lot/ no uh uh/
we didn't know nothin bout no party/
bobby started lookin at me yeah he started lookin at me
real strange/ like i waz a woman or somethin/
started talkin real soft in the back seat of that ol buick/

WOW
by daybreak/ i just cdnt stop grinnin

Leslie Silko

The white men who came to the Laguna Pueblo Reservation and married ,aguna women were the beginning of the half-breed Laguna people like my amily, the Marmon family. I suppose at the core of my writing is the attempt o identify what it is to be a half-breed or mixed blooded person; what it is to ;row up neither white nor fully traditional Indian. It is for this reason that I esitate to say that I am representative of Indian poets or Indian people, or ven Laguna people. I am only one human being, one Laguna woman.

I attended the University of New Mexico and graduated in 1969. I went to aw school at the University of New Mexico in the American Indian Law 'rogram for three semesters before I dropped out to devote all my time to vriting. I have a son, Robert, who was born in 1966 and another son, ;azimir, who was born in 1972. Presently I am teaching at the University f New Mexico in Albuquerque after several years in Ketchikan, Alaska.

WHEN SUN CAME TO RIVERWOMAN

that time
   in the sun
   beside the Rio Grande.

Voice of the mourning dove
   calls long ago long ago
   remembering the lost one
   remembering the love.
Out of the dense green
                    eternity of springtime
Willows rustle in the blue wind
          timeless
                the year unknown
                    unnamed.
The muddy fast water
   warm around my feet
   you move into the current slowly
Brown skin thighs
          deep intensity
          flowing water.
Your warmth penetrates
          yellow sand and sky

Endless eyes shining always
   for green river moss
   for tiny water spiders
Crying out
   the dove
          will not let me forget
   it is ordained
          in swirling brown water
          and it carries you away,
                my lost one
                my love
             in the mountain
man of Sun
                came to riverwoman

and in the sundown wind
he left her
to sing
for rainclouds swelling
in the northwest sky
for rainsmell on
pale blue winds
from China.

HORSES AT VALLEY STORE

Everyday I meet the horses
With dust and heat they come
step by step
Pulling the day
behind them.

At Valley Store
there is water.
Gray steel tank
Narrow concrete trough.

Eyes that smell water,
In a line one by one
moving with the weight of the sun
moving through the deep earth heat
They come.

People with
water barrels
in pick-ups in wagons
So they pause and from their distance
outside of time
They wait.

PREPARATIONS

Dead sheep
  beside the highway.
Belly burst open
    guts and life unwinding on the sand.

The body is carefully attended.
Look at the long black wings
      the shining eyes
Solemn and fat the crows gather
      to make preparations.

  Pull wood from skin
  Pick meat from bone
    tendon from muscle.
Only a few more days
    they say to each other
A few more days and this will be finished.

  Bones, bones
  Let wind polish the bones.
  It is done.

TOE'OSH: A LAGUNA COYOTE STORY

(for Simon Ortiz, July, 1973)

1

In the wintertime
at night
we tell coyote stories
                and drink Spanada by the stove.
How coyote got his
ratty old fur coat
            bits of old fur
            the sparrows stuck on him
            with dabs of pitch.

That was after he lost his proud original one in a poker game.
anyhow, things like that
are always happening to him,
that's what she said, anyway.

And it happened to him at Laguna
and Chinle
and at Lukachukai too, because coyote got too smart for his own good.

2

But the Navajos say he won a contest once.
It was to see who could sleep out in a
snow storm the longest
and coyote waited until chipmunk badger and skunk were all
curled up under the snow
and then he uncovered himself and slept all night
inside
and before morning he got up and went out again
and waited until the others got up before he came
in to take the prize.

3

Some white men came to Acoma and Laguna a hundred years ago
and they fought over Acoma land and Laguna women, and even now
some of their descendants are howling in
the hills southeast of Laguna.

4

Charlie Coyote wanted to be governor
and he said that when he got elected
he would run the other men off
the reservation
and keep all the women for himself.

5

One year
the politicians got fancy
at Laguna.

They went door to door with hams and turkeys
and they gave them to anyone who promised
to vote for them.
On election day all the people
stayed home and ate turkey
and laughed.

6

The Trans-Western pipeline vice president came
to discuss right-of-way.
The Lagunas let him wait all day long
because he is a busy and important man.
And late in the afternoon they told him
to come back again tomorrow.

7

They were after the picnic food
that the special dancers left
down below the cliff.
And Toe'osh and his cousins hung themselves
holding each other's tail in their mouth making a coyote chain
until someone in the middle farted
and the guy behind him opened his
mouth to say "What stinks?" and they
all went tumbling down, like that.

8

Howling and roaring
Toe'osh scattered white people
out of bars all over Wisconsin.
He bumped into them at the door
until they said
'Excuse me'
And the way Simon meant it
was for 300 or maybe 400 years.

Gary Soto

I was born on the night of April 12, 1952, in Fresno, California. Actually I was born at dusk -- yes, that's better. I was raised in South Fresno which is now factories, burned trees, spilled oil, and all that goes with urban renewal.

I attended Catholic and public schools, and always hid in the back rows of the classroom so as not to be called on by the teacher. I loved recess.

In the years 1970-74 I applied for food stamps and went to Fresno State where I took writing classes from Philip Levine, alias the Spanish dog, and Leonard Adame. In the meantime I was seeing a fine lady who fed and clothed me, and whom later I married.

Currently I'm working toward an MFA in creative writing at UC-Irvine. I've finished a manuscript entitled *Elements of San Joaquin* and am working on other poems. I was among the winners of the *YMHA Discovery - The Nation Award* for 1975 and won the *Academy of American Poets Prize* at UC-Irvine.

TOWN

When you looked back
The blind whose pupils were just visible
Under a whiteness, and yet
Fading like twin stars,
Opened their hands

And you turned away.
The town smelled of tripe
Pulled from an ox
And hanging --
Smoke, fruit wrinkling
Or bearded with gnats.
The streets shone with rain.

After the rain
You wore the heat like a shirt,
You drank until your mouth
Hung open and no longer
Bothered to shrug off
The flies.

Later you laid under a slow fan.
You got up
To watch from the window.
A dog snapped
The ankle of a woman
Carrying bricks. She kicked it
And went on.

Again you turned away
Afraid to think that it was night
And with the poor
You would sleep with spiders,
Dust in your throat
And sliding down.

HOEING

During March while hoeing long rows
Of cotton
Dirt lifted in the air
Entering my nostrils
And eyes
The yellow under my fingernails

The hoe swung
Across my shadow chopping weeds
And thick caterpillars
Who shriveled
Into rings
And went where the wind went

When the sun was on the left
And against my face
Sweat the sea
That is still within me
Rose and fell
From my chin
Touching land
For the first time

FIELD POEM

When the foreman whistled
My brother and I
Shouldered our hoes,
Leaving the field.
We returned to the bus
Speaking
In broken English, in broken Spanish
The restaurant food,
The tickets to a dance
We wouldn't buy with our pay.

From the smashed bus window,
I saw the leaves of cotton plants
Like small hands
Waving good-bye.

REMEMBER

Remember that we are moving away brother
From those years
In the same house with a white stepfather
What troubled him has been forgotten

But what troubled us has settled
Like dirt
In the nests of our knuckles
And can not be washed away

All those times you woke shivering
In the night
From a coldness I
Could not understand
And cupped a crucifix beneath the covers

All those summers we hoed our yard
In the afternoon sun
The heat waving across our faces
And we waved back wasps
While the one we hated
Watched us from under a tree and said nothing

We will remember those moments brother

And now that we are far
From one another
What I want to speak of
Is the quiet of a room just before daybreak
And you next to me sleeping

Thulani Nkabinde

Born Hampton, Va., 1949. Went to Barnard College, NYC. Formerly a reporter; researcher; director poetry workshop Black Writers Workshop, San Francisco, California; college instructor. Awarded *Lenore Marshall Prize for Poetry* (1970). Has started Isis/Oshun Productions with Ntozake Shange to publish books, scripts, etc. Published in *Black Creation, New American Poets, Third World Women, Umbra, Time to Greez, Jambalaya* & several black music record liners.

Statement on Poetics

Poetry is commitment & sound. Mine is an attempt at honesty/ at sound/ & usually betrays the fact that I'm an idealist & believe in black folks visions, as I've said before.

LIKE FIRE SPREADIN/THE JOYLESSNESS

soft thoughts ease on down
soft thoughts & old scenes
spread like wings & cognac
& shadow the bright blight of days
& smell & work
the old age of hope
moves slow out thru night eaves
i will be left to hang a non-ness
as a drifting used wish
granted or denied/ outgrown
like fire spreadin/ the joylessness
soon takes all & leaves the quick
eatin memory too bright to hold in eyes
the joylessness
like rushing up the street
to a lover who does not love you
the helplessness
of rushing still
the joylessness
of taking a lover & love
without loving
or having a reason
the helplessness
of comfort
the joylessness
of having beauty in parts & in time
the helplessness
of memory
of being in the wind/ without a howl

FOREST GREEN

today is forest green
light beige, dark brown
i'm singin my song
my song for you

today is autumn
i feel leaves, i feel wool
i feel changin color
i see the lake, your plants
hear your tune
it's movin, movin easy now
yemaya throw her right foot behind her left
step & glide those hips for you
teach ya to take a thought & sway
take a tear & hit it on high
hold it & laugh my skirts roun your thighs
yemaya got kalimba eyes
sing her song for you
grab you roun the waist
throw your cares behind your hip
push & knock em around a bit & be gone!
a little shy but terrible she dawn her touch of red
satin shoes step with you to dreams
& sing forest green
keep you heart for me
step up & be the man for me
keep your heart as free as can be for me
i hide my tears & sing for you
be with me awhile
i been taken off in desire's whirlwinds
lost to a song you cannot hear
let me spin by you
weave the tune for you
yemaya she in forest green

SONG FOR THE NKAZI OR THE FINAL IRONIES

"i'll get out of your life," i said.
"so??" she said.
"i will sip plum wine & take no bets on defying gravity
or other cosmic laws. there is universal time.
the go-roun will take me," i said.
"the winds move past my house & love enwraps me," she said.
"yes, love grows like a palm spurnin shade," i said.

"and so??" she said.
"we share the night flight & different directions.
i search the king cause the prince was busy. some have needed
me to learn to want. i am wanted on the far corners & need on
the near ones. wanting has gone down for wanting to want.
night flight will cover all quarters & take no bets," i said.
"the sun beams through my windows & love casts no shadows," she
"yes, love is a breathin kind of substance. only people cast
shadows & have darkness pacin behind them. love does not," i said
"i live where the hills kiss the loving and i get what i
desire," she said.
"i kiss the one who asks & love the one i'm with. even isis knew
loyal don't mean lucky. i bleed a queen's blood but take no bets
on my life," i said.

***

i wrapped the veil upon my head & across my face.
with kohl drawn about my eyes i disappeared into the throng,
or into the light of campfires & winds of wayfarers
into the midnight tales of those who have no home but their lives.
i pose as a wise woman who thinks of beauty
and is sometimes taken for evil
i am the old creature/ the one who is selfish
filled with words to her throat/ words which must have company
rather than go lonely to the air she shouts them in
the creature shouts mad/angry upon the earless desert
she wishes for the words a home
yet lets them barge in upon her heart
her tales are old/long told/ the creature repeats
we must all have a past to enhance the present
the creature repeats,
"i had one gifts, i thought to share
but to be received, it had to be taken from me.
it is the only way love can be taught to some."

ACCRA 8/75

(for the Poet/Gylan Kain)

I wander through
and I'm trying to touch you
eyes made like glass on me
never moving
we are silent
it is your way and I have no tongue
I had to see you/ Afrikans
I had to touch/ the connection
you join my visible image
my style upon the street
on this your land/ so understood
there is no inch you have to give
on this/ it's your land
& giving is not too much
it is yours
all I have is a ticket to a place
that I ain't taking or giving
& a style to survive it
I cannot give the ticket
nor share the wealth
pass the style & know the word
is all I do

MISSING MS

the burglars stole my love story
the only one i've been in
snuck the sequin sweat joy
& tear-eyed revelations out the window
conversation in bare wood rooms
all the unfinished home & marriage
went out with sneaker night feet
in the arms of men too young
for love more subtle than leg
hanging out the open car ride of spring.

Alma Villanueva

I grew up in San Francisco with my grandmother, mother and aunt; sometimes living together, sometimes separately -- mainly I stayed with my grandmother. I never liked school (everytime I'd check in they'd be doing the same thing) and my grandmother liked my company, so I stayed out and did things like visit China(town) and drink tea and eat fortune cookies, while other kids just read about it. My grandmother was from Sonora, Mexico and spoke both Yaqui and Spanish and she loved to recite poetry in her beautiful voice. My grandfather was a minister and ran his own newspaper. He was thrown out of his country for political reasons and was too proud to return, even when it was safe. He died in his early fifties. My aunt tells me when he would get out of the tub he'd say, "I smell of the best Mexican soil after a rain!" My grandfather, I am told, also wrote poetry -- it must be in my blood...my writing is my song to life -- it's taken me awhile to be able to hear it.

I am now living in Sebastopol, California, with David and our (combined) five kids. My oldest, my daughter Toni, is fifteen (I had her at fifteen) and the youngest is 6. We are eating our own meat, vegetables and eggs these days. I think my grandmother would like it here; she'd probably grow a lot of onions, chilis and cilantro.

TO JESUS VILLANUEVA, WITH LOVE

my first vivid memory of you
mamacita,
we made tortillas together
yours, perfect and round
mine, irregular and fat
we laughed
and named them: ose, pajarito, gatito.
my last vivid memory of you
   (except for the very last
   sacred memory
   i won't share)
mamacita,
beautiful, thick, long, gray hair
the eyes gone sad
with flashes of fury
when they wouldn't let you
have your chilis, your onions, your peppers
   --what do these damned gringos know of MY stomach?--*
so when I came to comb
your beautiful, thick, long, gray hair
as we sat for hours
(it soothed you
my hand
on your hair)
I brought you your chilis, your onions, your peppers.
and they'd always catch you
because you'd forget
and leave it lying open.
they'd scold you like a child
and be embarrassed like a child
silent, repentant, angry
and secretly waiting for my visit, the new supplies
we laughed at our secret
we always laughed
            you and I

you never could understand
the rules
at clinics, welfare offices, schools
any of it.
I did.
you lie. you push. you get.
I learned to do all this by
the third clinic day of being persistently
sent to the back of the line by 5 in the afternoon
and being so close to done by 8 in the morning.
so my lungs grew larger
and my voice got louder
and a doctor consented
to see an old lady,
and the welfare would give you the money
and the landlady would remember to spray for cockroaches
and the store would charge the food till the check came
and the bank might cash the check if I got the nice man this time
and I'd order hot dogs and cokes for us
at the old 'Crystal Palace' on Market Street
and we'd sit on the steps
by the rear exit, laughing
                        you and I

mamacita,
I remember you proudly at Christmas
time, church at midnight services:
you wear a plain black dress
your hair down, straight and silver
(you always wore it up
tied in a kerchief,
knotted to the side)
your face shining, your eyes clear,
your vision intact.
you play Death.
you are Death.
you quote long stanzas from a poem I've long
forgotten;

even fitful babies hush
such is the power of your voice,
your presence
fills us all.
the special, pregnant
silence.
eyes and hands lifted up
imploringly and passionately
the vision and power
offered to us,--
eyes and hands cast down
it flows through you
to us,
a gift.

your daughter, my mother
told me a story I'd never
heard before:
    you were leaving Mexico
    with your husband and two
    older children, pregnant
    with my mother.
    the U.S. customs officer
    undid everything you so
    preciously packed, you
    took a sack, blew it up
    and when he asked about
    the contents of the sack,
    well, you popped it with
    your hand and shouted
        MEXICAN AIR!*

aiiiiiiiii mamacita, Jesus,
I won't forget my visions and reality.
to lie, to push, to get
just isn't
enough.

* translated from Spanish; she refused (and pretended not to be able) to speak English.

UNTITLED

they didn't get me.
I feel like the hunted prey that
escaped

schools
churches
office jobs
city streets
morals
anglo culture/ western civilization/ the democratic process
dutiful sex free sex no sex
9-5
the perfect mother
    &   "   wife
I.Q.s/ M.D.s/ Ph.D.s/ U.S.A.
delivery rooms with drs. in a hurry
project walls a 1/2 inch thick
white kids who hate black kids
black kids who hate white kids
mexican kids who hate light kids
people who hate themselves & hate everyone

the city was the hunter
and the streets of my childhood were
peopled with many like me
   the streets soaked up
oil & blood & rain & tears & dog shit & footsteps & love &
children games & lives & piss & stunted trees & the blossoming
trees on Guerrero St & the hardy weeds that burst through
the cracks in spring, especially spring,
and the people, the people, the people

they told us in school one
time that a beautiful creek
ran down Dolores St and that on
Noe St indians fished for their supper, we were told
   can't you just see cornfields
spreading all over the Mission?

and all that time
the earth wasn't confined
to backyards and fences and the 'country'
   the weeds kept telling
me something I couldn't hear
the earth was laughing and listening and singing
all that time -- all our destruction
can't touch it. it lies in wait.

they can't touch us.
they didn't get us.

under my flesh/ this skin
my heart keeps pumping
   my blood
      laughing and listening and singing inside me
   all on its own
and I'm amazed.

UNTITLED

you cannot leave
my aunt's house
without a
full stomach
   she would be
   offended;
she's small
and earth color, her
face records
her mother's people
   the hills and desert of Sonora.
her eyes hold
an eclipse
   of clarity/pain:
      once,
         when I was small
   I remember
      her and I eating
         a cluster of grapes

in a matter of minutes
each one so delicious
we couldn't wait
for the next, and
when the last
grape was gone
we laughed because
the grape:s skeleton
looked so funny --
before she was born
her father recognized
her mother and converted (he was a minister)
and married her; his indian
blood mixed with that
of the spanish
conqueror. I saw a
picture of his congregation
in Mexico, his wife's brother
holding their first born
who died before five,
and the majority of his
followers indian/eyes stared
out at me and I
recognized them,
my aunt, not yet born
among them.

I grew up hearing
my aunt's visions and dreams,
she had no one but
a child to tell them to --
she saw the bombing
of Japan and the
back of God
and a neighbor's son opened
the front door and called her
the day he was reported missing
in action, and she
dreamt my house and knew

where the trees stood before
she ever came -- and she's
always apologetic for staying
'too long' and she's always
sorry you're leaving 'too soon' --
   talking and telling in spanish
to english
in english for the skeleton
in spanish for the flesh
we sit for hours
   she being older for awhile
   I being oldest in my turn
taking turns as we've
always done --
and she tells me
she tried going to
an anglo church, but their
faces were blank
and their
eyes
mute; they did not
recognize her --
and with the spontaneity of
a laugh held long
within her
   she smiles
as she tell mes:
      --Mi gente son el color de la tierra.--*
and the clarity overshadows
the pain.

   and she lapses and offers
me a cup of coffee and I
drink it or she
will be
offended.

*My people are the color of the earth.

UNTITLED

there were times
you and I
were hungry
in the middle of a city of
full bellies
   and we ate bread with
syrup on top and we joked
and said we ate dessert morning
noon & night, but
we were hungry --
so I took some bottles to the
store and got milk and
stole deviled ham because
it had a picture of the devil
on it and I didn't care --
   my favorite place
      to climb
         and sit was
            Devil's Rock
         no one else
            would sit there, but
               it was the
                  highest place
                     around --
taking care
of each other,
an old lady and a child
being careful
not to need
more than can be
given.
   we sometimes went to the
place where the nuns lived and
on certain days they would
give us a bag of food, you
and the old Mexican nun talking,
you were always gracious;

and yet their smell of dead
flowers and the rustle of their robes
always made me feel
shame: I would rather
steal.

   and when you held my bleeding nose
for hours, when I'd become
afraid, you'd tell me
          -- Todo se passa. --*

after you died I learned
to ride my bike to the ocean
   I remember the night
      we took the '5 McCallister'
         to the ocean and it was
            storming and frightening
   but we bought frozen chocolate bananas
      on a stick and ate them
         standing, just you and I
            in the warm, wet night --
and sometimes I'd wonder why
things had to pass and I'd
have to run as fast as I could
till my breath wouldn't let me
or climb a building scaffold to the
end of its steel or
climb Rock Mountain and
sit on Devil's Rock
and dare the devil
to show his face
or ride my bike till the
end of the streets hit
sand and became ocean
and I knew
the answer, mamacita, but
I wouldn't even say it to
myself.

*Everything passes.

grandmother to mother to
daughter to my daughter,
the only thing that truly
does not pass is
love --
and you
knew it.

Ron Welburn

Born 30 April, 1944, Bryn Mawr, Pennsylvania. Grew up in Philadelphia. Attended Lincoln University (Pa) with poets S.E. Anderson, F.J. Bryant, Carl H. Greene, Steve Wilmore and Gil Scott-Heron. M.A. from University of Arizona. Taught at Syracuse University from 1970-1975. Poems in several anthologies and journals, *Peripheries: Selected Poems 1966-1968* published by Greenfield Review Press in 1972. In fifth year of waiting for two volumes of verse accepted by other publishers. Was a fellow in Jazz criticism with the Music Critics Institute in summer, 1975. Is married and lives in Brooklyn. Has warm memories of the Third World Writers Workshop at Stevens Point -- a beautiful community.

DELIA DALYA OF THE SPONGED STILTS

("your mom wear high-heeled sneakers!"
"your mom wear high-heeled sneakers!")

the strung along cities
are a fuzzbox filled with mindless claims
the senses we wear
don't belong to we
belong to the master switcher
ji-roo, aint it hip! switch
ji-roo, ah, hip! switch,
and switch on, now

("yo mom wear high-heeled sneakers!"
"yo mom wear elevator shoes to work!")

and now we in stilt country
ste staves pinching the walking asses
that switch
ji-roo
bobbing like snipes;
people looking like orthopedic dancers
woman leans forward and
stalks up and down
could scare frankenstein away
or chase nightmare off to the woolly hills
look like the shoe of the cloven foot-hoof
to me
I said: look like the heel of the cleft
footprint stuffed up with sty-pen mush to me!

("your mom, and her high-heeled sneakers!"
"your daddy wear ladder boots to bed!")

coming down the street
fisheye figures in elephant pantaloons
o, stash and style!
coming down the fisheyed funneled street
coming down wearing the lens
walking their extension cord bodies
too big or too small for the striding boots

("mom wear high-heeled tennis shoes!"
"you look like you standin' on a train platform!"
"if you tilt, baby, you'll fall off the scaffold!")

we here in the electra land
of apocalyptic bootery
fred braun's and I.J. miller, flaggs and do,
trapeze to the bank.
(I used to run around happykid
in sneakers, high-topped my folks
made me wear, until I saved my pennies
and bough me some converses, jim! ----- solid!)

("your mom wear high-topped sneakers!"
"your mom wear high-heeled sneakers!")

I am a freak
in a world of stilt eaters and talkers,
napoleonic complexes in high voltage
look me over fisheye to eye.
when I've been drinking, or feel like
being malicious, I dream I am
a fisherman, with stilt fish in my net
their bellies up and their backs on a bygone age.
it's very peaceful by this pool,
except for that high nasal voice in the distance

("your mom wear high-heeled sneakers!!")

HOPES ARE FULL OF BLISTERS

hopes of night places
and faces are full of blisters
we sweatin out dis hyere liberation
ting in the evening yard
mowing another's lawn

picked cotton all day and
sing songs nightime abrasive
clods flying in the air
in the wind those latins we think
happier than we
are in their rhythms and shoes
designed for thin ankles
life is stranger than science
and sometimes fiction
life is learning and sometimes
even stronger than
drums are ancestral voices
calling
calling
telling
calling
and are starting to get
the blisters from
our hands.

ATTICA

picked up where
dachau left its mark
this civilization
brothers enguarded have their
bodies luxury of stews
their meat savoring palettes
of the wealthy
and the armed

so they are closing down interment camps
so we all abide within circles of fire
oftener quick
draw lightning punctures our desperation
mood of men and machines
alive it is a waste who
are mated poverty and pain

we are enough within walls
to be leaders of such burials
still gone unnoticed in the news
these wastes sanctified in sabbaths

if there is no light or bulb
in the heart building the wall
if there is no future
when you live scurvied in filth allowed
take the lessons most dear
manifest the survival urge
fittest though downed.

DOG DREAM

(for Walt Shepperd)

there can be no end where
beginnings are caught
in the dog's mouth, chased,
and then permitted to fall
in a line at the rear of its eyes,
or wave back and forth
like some kind of banner
advertising vitamins or warm homes.

packs of wild hounds track
through my sleep, their nails
telegraph against the wood.
walt called it a medieval scene,
and there are more of them than us.
they run around the neighborhoods
looking for something, stopping
for a fight or a screw, defecating
on lawns. they are running around looking,
and maybe soon, they'll find
someone to eat.

there can be no beginning where
ends are caught
in the dog's mouth, sucked on,
and bitten off.
it will drag the floor
focused in blood
and there will be screams
as from human throats,
and we will be caught unawares
when those eyes look into our souls,
and they are getting ready for the leap.

BURGUNDY PHASE

a cap for night and
a cap for winter

a striding of trousers and
a sweater to giraffe my neck

mirrors and other viewers
capture the countenance
of my woolen fezzed crown

I am a griot
my instrument in periodic silence
I am a keeper of oxen
or a trader, I will exchange
poems listlessly for money

maroon or burgundy
I sip the juice of fabrics and dare
look dashing in my mellow pace of the day
it is burgundy as phase I am in
come around from green or brown

I bleed under the clouds
like the inverted moon of a woman
who is dry for a week
my cap strident stop my hair
I am playing the wise man
to the hilt just as I was told
by my comrades years ago
my burgundy is
the rubiyat's wine and the
passion of allah

burgundy mingles
with my choice of poem
and dictates the essence
of my song

burgundy done gone to my head
burgundy, gone to my head and shoulders
burgundy, going to my legs and feet
burgundy, as if borrowed from
a sagittarian princess
for me.

VISION OF MONTEZUMA PRESERVE, N.Y.

dead trees
pock-mark the marsh
white hairs on the chest
of an old sentinel

a city looms behind them
naked of cultures
stones hang from the neck
pushed as we go forth

owl sits on a bristled stalk

the city is vermin

owl coughs up
knotted pieces of my brother.

Shawn Wong

Shawn Wong is one of the co-editors of *Aiiieeeee! An Anthology of Asian American Writers* (Doubleday) and *Yardbird Reader* volume 3. He is a co-director of The Combined Asian American Resources Project, Inc. (CARP) and an instructor at San Francisco State University. When he is not at work plodding along in the eighth version of his novel, he dabbles in areas which he has no expertise, such as: playing the bus boy in his own television drama for children to be aired this fall in a series called *Vegetable Soup* (NBC and PBS-TV), directing Frank Chin's play *The Chicken coop Chinaman* for The Oakland Museum Theatre (March 1975), and uttering those memorable lines in the television movie, *Farewell to Manzanar* (directed by John Korty), "When are we going to get some sugar?"

FROM KICKING LEGO BLOCKS

1.

Two hours after I saw her
at 2 a.m., June 28th, 1972
Cindy sat down to write to me,
"So much to do
I had to push aside paper piles
and write this to you."

And it was all of me
in the poem.

And I also went home
at midnight after seeing you
to write back to you
to say something about my father
because you put me back in touch
with myself
left me thinking and seeing
a dream out of the clear night
until it started raining
and you were home
giving me the day
as it comes from the heart
so full of sun
even writing about the day:

"The dogs are barking
I must go outside into the sun bleached day now
Kicking Lego blocks and mini trucks from steps,
To tug on dry crackling grass with clawing roots
From around my big wooden house
Before that fire next time."

This is only the beginning
and you watch me now
as I make my life up from friends
what they've given me.

And I'm always driving,
pulling myself up by my arms
to see and create
to chronicle everything that I am
for you
so that you will see me growing.

II.

Wherever we are in this country
you and I are still thinking
about each other.
Cindy in Miami, San Diego,
even from Vienna you wrote to me.

I was in the mountains
always sending postcards
from places I've never been to before.
And maybe someday we'll
be in the same place together
sending cards home
from some windy place
from some home that gives
our families to us
from old old buildings where we used to live
from an island
where you are taking me
to show me where your grandmother survived

where you'll say to me
that all she wanted was a place to live
and you'll show me a window
that I can look out
and see my own home
and hear nothing except the broken glass
under your shoes
keeping time with your voice saying,
"We'll make them all remember I swear,
We'll stake out this place and unleash the ghosts."

The windows are broken and open
for Cindy's ghosts to fly through
tearing the sill to shreds.
No splinters come from this rotting wood
Cindy passes through
and walks lightly to hear
voices rise up to greet her
like me listening for my father's voice
move through the floor
at the radio station
Cindy becomes blind
to hear only
to run her fingers across
poems
carved into the walls
with fingers like Cindy's.
"Staying on this island
My sorrow increases with the days
My face is growing sallow
And my body is getting thin
Cooped up here, my difficulties are unending
Now, I dare to give up all and go back."
We will never go back
We will root ourselves in place
on this land
Cindy will see to it
because these buildings breathe
because this whole island is a heart
beating
"Ask the Indians they'll all tell you,"
Cindy says,
"that an island is the saddest
kind of land there is."
We do unleash ghosts now
that fill all the homes
and Cindy still cries
but she's mad now
so we take hold
of this stronghold
to chronicle all that is rising
up to greet us
in Cindy's fire

VIII.

Breakfast at Cindy's place
is full of smiles
like Marty marching off to school
with his briefcase,
the dogs are crying
at his leaving
and we are left alone in your house
to realize that Marty goes off
to do so many things at school
with his life
and we're at home
relaxed, talking projects,
making moves to control what we do
while Marty grabs what he sees
protects what he learns
uses what he learns
to create everything that he will be.

And we are already
recording things
making lists of what we have been
or what we will be to each other
to our friends
or even, to nations of people
we don't even know.

But the music is on
And Cindy is making
Italian enchiladas filled with Spam
sprinkled with cheese
for breakfast,
hot Viennese Blend coffee,
and after breakfast
we have Cindy's omelet bread
made with chicken and duck eggs
from the coop,
macaroons the size of fists,
and San Miguel Beer
to ruin the rest of the day.

By June 1972
Cindy had written that poem for me
knowing me only three months
and I wrote back a month later
giving Cindy my poem for her
in a letter saying,
"Dear Cindy, I have finished your poem.
I struggled to see the vision that holds the poem,
but breaks the person --
excuse me if I have given you a harsher vision
or a harsher dream about the children
of Southeast Asia than you might have.
It makes the point.
There are certain problems
with the poem that I will work out
in the next few weeks;
(1) 'red clouds' interrupts
the images of blue,
and (2) I am wondering if 'commitment'
just before is strong enough."

I must have known Cindy longer
to know that wasn't strong enough
in fact, nothing *said* is strong enough
only the working
the *doing*
matters to Cindy
and so I looked back at what I said
about Cindy
about all that love among friends
and still felt what I said
mattered because it was for Cindy.
I looked back to March 25, 1971
when Kay dedicated a poem for me,
with love, saying,
"Once into this curse of reading, one learns there are places
Named My Song, My Lai, and also the other tramplings to death,

The assault upon leaves, roots, small vines with their palms open..."
I never corrected the poem for Cindy
but wrote back to her
on September 16, 1972
to say something I had been feeling
all along:
"...your simple note settled me,
nothing to jump for joy about,
or anything that obvious,
or gaudy,
but a happiness surrounded by simplicity
that is implied in the definition of the action,
Kindness.
Ever, ever is another word
that moves like a song
exposes the heart in its tone,
never hides, never patronizes.
The word speaks directly, creates form,
has its own voice.
Now I am telling you that words
speak for themselves,
out of control.
But ever is stronger than commitment."

Now I have put all of that
into the story about me
the long work
about a home on the range
that is mine
that is everything my heart wants
and together we never
needed much
because we were always
giving something to each other

Cindy has always
given me small cups, pots,
shirts, food,
useful things
like we were in exile together
needing supplies
like letters

Like now
to build
to carve
all that we want
at the marrow
where our blood clings
where it will pulse out of the bone
when needed
to invade an island
of people we knew,
to protect friends,
to find words like genocide
come pulsing out of our mouths
in a voice strong
as the bone it flows from
because we've seen children
wear their flesh like loose clothing.
Maybe they're all dead now
and maybe the children still there
will die from a war
that still goes on

within them
because they're still looking
for homes, for food,
that will take years to grow
out of their own land
but Cindy will continue to cry
over some soldier-father
who died years ago
simply because he missed his family
his life continues for her
will come back to her
especially on hot days like today

when I can see Cindy
down on her hands and knees
pulling dry crackling weeds
from around her home
"Before that fire next time."
But it was always,
yes, always
Cindy's fire.

LOVE AMONG FRIENDS

In trust you showed me a photograph
of a ragged girl with long black hair
cradling a wounded baby.
She pretends to whisper rhymes to her sister
saying all the time, "Renew these bones."
Calmly, you tell me that there are places
where children
have learned to lie down like tigers
and watch for the fire,
the blue fire.

Then you asked me to understand your spirit
because of love among friends.
To carry the wounded children,
to cradle their blue arms in mine.
Spring passes by in a moment of dreams
and we too have learned to sleep like tigers
to watch for the fire that is precious
blue and ceaselessly blue.

Being a mother you said
that you would pay for everything
not in guilt, but by commitment.
You must dream at night of your own
children lost in a world of red clouds.

This is not tragedy, do not concern yourself
with the children's fear,
they have seen nothing else, never sleep
long enough for dreams.
There are places like the Plain of Jars to dream about,
and there are cold, restless places to sleep in.

ELEGY FOR A GREENHOUSE

(For Arthur Okamura)

Okamura's greenhouse fell down today
his colored cows were munching on a field
of moonlit nasturtiums
and used the nails of the roof for toothpicks.
The moonlight strikes the cows
coloring them black
and moon.
Their sides glow like walking atlases
the moon white countries
lost in their black hide oceans.
The seesaw of greenhouse windows in the wind
and the crash is a voice saying,
"Japanese artists make bad gardeners!"
They let their gardens grow
out of sight
pruning and nurturing the roots.

Al Young

Al Young is the author of three books of poetry and three novels, including *Geography of the Near Past* (poems) and *Sitting Pretty* (fiction) which Holt brought out simultaneously in the spring of 1976. For some time now, he has lived and worked near San Francisco.

THE NEW MYSTIC

The waters I'm going to go walking beside,
vibrations I've been taking into my system,
the cool nourishing breeze,
the living browns & greeneries
waving in the wind around me,
the real men & women
with whom I keep in touch,
our souls poking out
like bone
thru serious wounds,
the basic familiar smell of life
raw or uncooked
breathed in thru nostrils
or exhaled thru tenderer membranes
-- proof flowing back to me
that there's only one Dreamer:
the playful faddist & mystery lover
who sees me thru these boogies & tangos
whose steps & movements
seem to get made up
somehow as I go along

TEACHING

There's no such thing as a student,
only abiding faces unwilling
to change except with time,
the oldest force that still fools us

So you teach a feeling,
a notion learned the hard way,
a fact, some figures,
a tract, some rigors of childhood

The face out there
interacting with yours
knows how to grin & play with its pen
but misses the point so charmingly

A thousand moves later
that same shiny face
moving thru the world with
its eyes glazed or fully closed
re-connects with one of its own childhoods

Loosely we call this learning

GEOGRAPHY OF THE NEAR EAST

The trick
without anyone
catching on to it
is to swim against
world current
knowing it is as much a dream
as it is drama on the highest stage
but without losing touch
with spirit or with light

Realer even
is to move as if
nothing has ever happened
which is likewise
as true as foam or fog

Each universe is only
an ever shifting sea
in the surfacing eyes of former fish

Lorraine Sutton

I am Puerto Rican and female. A major portion of my writing is born from this reality, but not confined to it. In my first book of poems *SAYcred LAYdy* (Sunbury Press), New York/ Puerto Rico

rhythms/ sadness
anger
love hunger
struggle &
freedom

are parts that
make up my voice -- a RAW & active
Borinqueña
voice.

I was born in Caguas, Puerto Rico on November 9, 1949. Soon after I was brought to N.Y. Though having lived most of my life in Manhattan I spent my summers and schooling in the South Bronx. From there came the experiences that found themselves on paper in 1973. In that same year I received the Lehman College Grace A. Croff Poetry Prize. Since then I have published in various mags including *Sunbury/El Tiempo/West End/Best Friends/ & Ms. Magazine.* I am presently living in THE BRONX where I conduct poetry owrkshops for children, work to stay alive, give readings in & out of nueva york, do editorial work for *Sunbury* magazine...& squeeze an extra hour out of 24...to work on my second volume of poems to be titled *Roots.*

ROOTS

some people make fun
of my pain
my anger
who do i think
i am anyway
writing about
Ricans
& what does Caguas
mean to me anyway?

just a poor town
in an island
where i was spit out
& given
to some woman
who came by
& felt sorry
for a baby
too young
to be a servant
too much trouble
for a family
of seven

in New York
another woman
saw me
loved me
brought me up
hiding in closets
til the investigator
left
she didn't want to
lose me
she loved me/fed me
clothed me

& the schools were
all catholic

i studied hard
i went to dance class
        for the only mother
        i knew
        raised on
        collared greens/
        pigs knuckles/
        hominy grits &
        rice   &
                beans

from 93 st/ 1526 madison ave
            fox street
hot broken summers in the
South bronx
                pure cold winters
                in manhattan
with a name
like sutton   the answers
                 get lost
                 in the questions
                 mud muddled
                 nothing is
                 black & white
                 there's always
                 an 'other'
                 am i an 'other'
                        mami?

she was
for years & years
from foundling home
to foster ones
back & forth
to   &   fro
too light to pass for black
                & vice versa
she struggled
she survived
              gave birth to her own
              & loved me even more
              lost

in three
worlds
the questions got longer
                    & harder
                    a motherless
                      mother for
                    a motherless
                      daughter
                    & the pain grew
                       the pain grew
                       deeper/darker

tales of Borinquen
swaying palm trees
boleros//jibaros
Caribbean beaches
dreams just dreams
                    & children cut me
                       with their
                       laughter

                'ju can't even spic
                  spanish girl'

the anger grew
inside the coconut milk
i never tasted
inside veins
of latin fire
a heritage
              swelled
                        bursting
                        into
Puerto Rican
flames of history
                    written by
                  American men

this is not a song of lament
i stopped that long ago
i stopped that when
        the maze began
        unravelling
        complicated questions
        with hard facts//
        fists SMASHING
        glass barriers
        no longer circling
        the 'other' circle
so..... if i jump & S CrEAMMM
        in pain
                it is a HOWWWWWL
        an affirmation
        of self
        of roots
        of roots UP ROOT TED
                uprooted
        & spread
                like wildfire
        across   two countries
                two languages
                two thoughts
                two schools
                too many years
                spent/wasted
and NOW
it is time to reclaim
my palm trees
it is time to reclaim
my air
my land
my I-sland
my Puerto Rico
                my self

IVAN SILEN P.R. POET

Poor Ivan
blurting profanity
after profanity
God is gone
love never was
bells replace balls
in New York
where statues replace people
behind
triple locks
behind
electrical gadgets
behind
Zenith
RCA
GE
behind
billions of colors
and dozens upon dozens
of grade "A" eggs
Oh Ivan
Poor Ivan
you are not white
you are
medium "B"
i feel where you burn
blistered skin
scabs of ancient pain
lost to humanity
forever
invisible
Ivan
i walk where you walk
i see what you see
i understand
i cry
i understand
i laugh

Crazy
such a big place New York
to be lost and found in
afraid and strong in
Poor Ivan
visions clouded
mine too
wrapped in dreams
of struggle
twisting wriggling
inside hot desert sands
go!   go!
racing a heat of blinding
yellow
swallowing drops of salt
ahead! ahead!
picturesque Caribbean beaches
in shades of blue and gold
mother
father
ice cold rum and coke
Poor Ivan
image shattered
mine too
again and again again
and again and again and
again
crushed
smashed
by Rockaway waves of human
filth
Poor Ivan
My   Ivan
your New York
love/hate
mine too
mine too

FOR LEON

and it all goes twirling around
as tho you never were/ never came-
to know what you do what you don't
is never explained until the wires
jerk wild & free yr tongue thick
agst false teeth like everything
else is hot and the jolts are waves
w/ supersonic hearing for some mad
scientist/doctor/freak who wants
to inject/inspect   come to
                                        grips

w/ self inside you

perspiring adverse reactions
jump-kick-swell while the hair falls
in thick clumps on the floor all
around you   outside yr cold clammy
sick wet hands

telephone wires short circuit yr
conversation w/yr brain
because yr lips don't make sounds
they move but they don't make
sounds
i want to hear you speak
i want to hear soundssoundssounds
if i punched you would you scream?
yr eyeballs are not wet
yr hair is almost gone
yr walk is weak   they've picked
you dry   yr lips   are cracked
yr tongue can't move around anymore

    you can't remember anymore
    you can't remember anymore

three a week/times 8 weeks/ makes
24 24 24 24 24 24
one for every year *in* yr life
one for every year of yr life

one for every year you can't remember

FOR MY BROTHER HENRY T. SUTTON JR.

what do you say to the voice
hysterical
crying
who can bear no longer
who refuses to accept
the pain of defeat
who is caught up in a web
of pain
and fire
her son burned
fully
in his youth
what do you say to the voice
depleting savings account
a woman's savings account
a puerto rican savings account
a Puerto Rican/woman/city worker
savings account
with no more to pay private nurses
. . . and they say she must pay
PAY PAY PAY for the body
that needs one to one care
for the body that was almost
ripped from her womb
for the flesh that can no longer
bear the unbearable pain
of not being free white &

21

what do you say to this
woman mother whose life
has been filled with
foundling home &
prostitution
& waitressing
& bitter smiles
& lonely years
endured in silence
in silent agony
in silent anger
feeling more respectable now
as a city worker
a city worker --
SINCE WHEN ARE CITY WORKERS
RESPECTED?
respected for their labor
for their years away from (their own)
children
respected for their hands
& minds that work
that must pay
that must pay
for anything & everything
they do not control
respected for the sweat
they put in
& the ruling few don't
since when is your mother
different than mine
woman hysterical crying
into ears
into ears that have spent
time listening
since when are workers
respected?
since when do you belong
to a privileged class
whose biggest sentence
is "go back where you came from"

my mother came from
yr ancestors sperm
my mother was born here
my brother was born here
they are both dying here
& she can never go back
& she can never go back
she can never go back
to the island that never
claimed her
to the ISLAND that is THEIRS
THEY
THEM
those who shape the world
on gasoline oil & EFCB
those who claim a foreign
nation for their own
in the name of MANIFEST DESTINY
those who wipe out an entire people's
culture...language...being
those who continue
to sing the star spangled banner
without realizing there isn't
any
ain't none
nothin'
to those i say
what do you say to this
woman mother
whose son
is slowly dying
inside a cadaver
someone else death
grafted to cover
the 85%
the 85%
scalded
burnt
destroyed
beyond
1st 2nd & 3rd
degree

burns
burns
skin
tissue
muscle
nerves
what
is
left
for this woman
but to watch
to cry
to SCREAM
@ those who pass
the buck from:
administrators
directors
supervisors
& SOCIAL WORKERS
who claim
who say
in 99 44/100% pure
anglish

'sorry honey this ain't
SOCIALized medicine'

what is left
for this
mother woman
but to ache
for the eyes that roll
back & forth
slipping in & out
of consciousness
tryin to lift
his bandaged arm
he my brother wants to
suck his thumb. . . .

he has no thumb
he has no arm
he has no face
he is invisible

what do you say to the voice
hysterical crying
for her 22 year old son
who died last sunday

Peter Blue Cloud

Peter Blue Cloud is an Akwesasne Mohawk. His books of poetry include *Kokopilau And Friend* (Blackberry Press) and *Turtle Bear And Wolf* (Akwesasne Notes Press). His work has appeared in many magazines, often under such pseudonyms as Coyote II and he was instrumental in the publication of the book *Alcatraz Is Not An Island.* A former poetry editor of "Akwesasne Notes," he is now living in Northern California. His newest collection of poetry *White Corn Sister* has been scheduled for publication in late 1977 by Strawberry Press.

STONE MOUNTAIN FACE

Charlie bends to feed the stove
dry oak, and the fire throws
a glow of red in early morning,
I take the pot of coffee and pour
our cups full, and the dog
thumps her tail upon the floor

her nose twitching in sleep
and from the odor of deerhide
soaking in a bucket, I roll
a smoke and we listen to
the steady beat of rain against
the roof and dripping to ground

"yes, I was thinking of the drum
we are trying to make
and trying to dream its shape
and sound, but the images weren't
clear at all, and the rain was
drumming all night, so I came
over to ask if you'd heard its
shape and sound yet",
Charlie
asked this, sipping coffee and
the firebox door was still open
and our shadows were quivering
giants across the floor and wall
and the sharp odor of ripe hide
stung the room, and I hesitated,

awhile, remembering a strange dream
mixed with the outdoor thru window
earlier visions of the night, of
lightning upright walking the
sagebrush land, electric-charged
walkers become outlines

of bright colored dancing, dancing
acrid puffs of power of feet
to ground, dancing a frenzy
across sand dunes to the west
toward the first low hills
of Storm Mountain, where clouds
of dark waters are born

and reflect themselves in the lake
of a tamarack village up there
in the midst of fir and cedar
where bear and deer wander, "no,
I heard no shape or sound but
saw a thing, a wonderous, though

frightening thing, I can't remember
just what it might be, a thought
of my own imagining, or something
I'm to know about later, maybe",
and Charlie looked at the hide
soaking, floating, staring
and
beckoned me with a hand,
I leaned toward the bucket
and looked, and then stared,
a shiver sort of at my neck
as I saw the twisted face the
folds of hide portrayed, and
"yes, I think that's what it

wants to be, and I guess we
have to do it." and right then
began a frantic pace to do
a thing we didn't know just
what or why, but knew only
that it was ours to do, and

don't
thank me hastily, the oak tree
whispered, as I cut slim branches,
and basket willow, too, hoped
I knew what it was all about, and
sapling maple thongs peeled
slippery singing, questioned my
fingers nervous haste, as rain
now slowed to drizzle waiting,
and four hands in a harmony
of expectation began to fashion
a hoop and frame, peeling and
bending and lashing fast with
swift, sure fingers.

then hands again in counter motion
twisting the deerhide to dryness,
the acrid odor dilating nostrils
and racing pulses, forcibly,
as does the blood smells of
fresh killed creatures.

and in a silence of concentration
we lashed the hide to frame
with a coiling lace of maple,
and cut, and inserted fingers
pulling, tearing, forcing
the shape of a face known,
uneven and crude, mouth
curled and open over hide teeth,
close to fire, the face was leaned,

then we pried open paint cans
and dipped with fingers, and
the face was given a lightning
flash of white, and streaking
dots of blue, and orange lips,
brown earth eye circles and
black night hollow cheeks,

Now long and flowing strands of maple
were tied to frame and knotted
then hide which was head
of the face we had fashioned.
and we looked at it only once,
finished and drying further
close to stove's heat,
    then
we drove to the leveling-off
place of Storm Mountain, close
to tamarack village, beneath an old
fir, there we stood the face, against
the mound of roots and tilted stone,
    and sat beneath a neighbor cedar,
to join the forming storm above
our heads, and maybe walked
about on stabbing lightning legs,
and the black and writhing clouds
were our stomachs in the mind
of storm thinking, as branches
    whipped in storm dance,
and saplings like grass in earth dance,
heads low to ground, backs arched,
in willing pain,
                        the drumming
of rainfingers to shivering branches,
the howling slapping wind,
                                        and
    the after calm,
    and two old men
                        bent with age
slowly
    making their way
    down Storm Mountain.

CROW

back and forth cawings between black,
wet trees and crows, early morning
joyful conversation, a light drizzle
accents the gleam of flapping wings,
    Spring scents the air
in promise   of green corn shoots
and the breeze carries a richness
of thawing soil and "caw"
and answering "caw" lift my body
upward
            and I flap mightily
to climb above the trees
and look over my shoulder
for one, last, joyous
                                "caw".

COYOTE'S SONG

"Grandfather Coyote, sing us a song."
"Yes, grandfather, tell us a story."
"How was it when you was little like us, grandfather?"

Coyote sat down and took his muddy tail between his hands, releasing beads of mud. He picked up a bit of mud and held it close to his eyes. "See, I'm cross-eyed and holding one bead but seeing two because I'm looking so close." He flicked the bead over his head, "Now it is behind me and rolling toward world's end, getting bigger and bigger. My inside eyes can see many more than two." He picked up other beads of mud and began rolling them into a ball.

"It was long before there was a beginning. Half-water-thing was arguing with sky-fish about who had the best swimming place. They always argued about this same thing, but this time they reached a decision; they would trade places and find out for themselves, and so they did.

"Sky-fish swam over to half-water-thing's round house when he got hungry and the old lady was stirring mush in there and just grabbed sky-fish and threw him in the fire. Her son would be hungry when he returned, she thought, and would like a baked sky-fish.

"Of course, the very same thing happened to half-water-thing, too." Coyote looked at the children, "they say that's why sky is always in water and water in sky. Still looking for those two that got baked." Coyote looked to the surrounding hills, looked far away; "Maker give our tribe all this land to swim around in. Pretty soon you kids gonna be going to different places and learning different things, like them others. Gonna get awful curious, too, and look around in their round houses. Hope you kids don't get thrown into the fire. Hate to see my grandchildren get baked."

The children were uncomfortable and squirmed around. They didn't like grandfather to be serious, they liked him better when he teased a little. Little grandson felt as they did. He grabbed older brother's tail and crouched behind it, pretending to hide from grandfather. He tried real hard and finally managed to cross his eyes. He tried to imitate grandfather's deep voice and very solemnly said, "Don't bake sky-fis, don't bake sky fis."

The children laughed at little grandson, then laughed harder when they saw grandfather laugh. He looked at little grandons, "Oh, yes, you are a coyote, no doubt," he said. "And now I'll sing you a song if one of you will get my gourd rattle." And when he took the rattle he began a soft, shushing rhythm. At first he spoke softly to the rhythm, "before there was a beginning, there was another beginning to join the old one. Before the sky-people there were the spirit people. The spirit people dreamed of night and sky, and the dream became real. This is the song:

now now now now
there has been a sleeping,
now now now now
there has been a dreaming,
now now now now
our sleep is of dreaming,
and in our dreaming,
we go back to the spirit
and we sleep with the spirit,
we go back to the spirit
and we sleep with the spirit,
now now now now . . . "

And grandfather Coyote sang this song four times, each time a little softer. And after the fourth time the children slept, and he kept the low shushing of the gourd going, as he gazed into the fire.

Picture Credits
Americo Casiano & Sandra Maria Esteves by Layle Silbert
Michael Harper by Shirley Harper
Nashira N'tosha by Jessica Tarahata Hagedorn
Simon Ortiz by Hilary Langhorst
Ricardo Sanchez by LaVerne H. Clark
Ntozake Shange by Don Mguyer
Gary Soto by Scott Bartlett
Thulani Nkabinde by Lew Harrison
Shawn Wong by John Yu
Al Young by Jim Marks